INSPIRED RETIREMENT LIVING

FIND PASSION AND PURPOSE WITH HOBBIES, CRAFTS,
AND ACTIVITIES FROM AROUND THE WORLD

GET 101 WAYS TO ENJOY RETIREMENT + 101 MORE WAYS
TO ENJOY RETIREMENT

RAVINA M CHANDRA

RMC PUBLISHERS

Copyright © 2023 by Ravina M Chandra

All rights reserved.

No part of this publication may be reproduced in any form, or by any means, electronic or mechanical, including photocopying, recording, or any information browsing, storage, or retrieval system, without prior permission in writing from the publisher.

Under no circumstance will any blame or legal responsibility be held against the publisher, or author, for any damages, reparation, or monetary loss due to the information contained within this book. Either directly or indirectly. You are responsible for your own choices, actions, and results.

Please note the information contained within this document is for educational and entertainment purposes only. All effort has been executed to present accurate, up to date, and reliable, complete information. No warranties of any kind are declared or implied. Readers acknowledge that the author is not engaging in the rendering of legal, financial, medical or professional advice. The content within this book has been derived from various sources. Please consult a licensed professional before attempting any techniques outlined in this book.

Published by RMC Publishers

ISBN 978-1-7386846-9-4 (Paperback)
ISBN 978-1-998186-10-5 (Hardcover)
ISBN 978-1-998186-00-6 (E-book)

www.ravinachandra.com

ALSO BY RAVINA M CHANDRA

In the *Inspired Retirement Living* Series

101 Ways to Enjoy Retirement Across America

Other books

The Art of Senior Dating
Longevity and Eating Habits
Your Life, Your Story

TABLE OF CONTENTS

101 WAYS TO ENJOY RETIREMENT

Introduction	3
1. UNITED KINGDOM	7
Visits to the seaside	8
Drinking, British style	9
Tea drinking	9
Go on a historical outing	10
Fine dining	11
Sightseeing and Photography	11
Take a further education course	12
Speakers' clubs	12
Summary	13
2. THAILAND	15
Soap carving	16
Yoga	18
Collecting amulets	19
Scuba diving	21
Thai cooking	22
Summary	23
3. BELGIUM	25
Hot-air ballooning	26
Ghost Hunting in Belgium	28
Garage sales	30
Patchwork fantasies	31
Jigsaws	33
Summary	34
4. FRANCE – L'HEXAGONE	35
The Tour de France	36
Boules or Pétanque	38

Champagne and chartreuse	40
Perfume	43
Boulevard life in Paris	44
Summary	45

5. CANADA — 47
Curling	48
Exploring with a camper van or RV	49
Pickleball	51
Little Free Libraries	52
Summary	54

6. GREECE — 55
Swimming in the sea	56
Tavli on the sidewalks	57
Olive appreciation	58
Ancient history & Mythology	59
Bird watching	60
Summary	61

7. NEW ZEALAND — 63
Eco gardening	64
Beekeeping	67
Canning	68
Board games	70
Book clubs	71
U3A	72
Choirs	73
Crochet clubs	74
Summary	75

8. GERMANY — 77
Tatort	78
River cruises	78
Geocaching	80
Toy voyagers	82
Garden gnomes	83
Summary	84

9. AUSTRIA	87
Theatre	88
Yodeling	90
Accordion playing	91
Jewelry making from scrap (or kits)	92
Summary	93
10. SINGAPORE	95
Journaling and blogging	96
Virtual reality	98
Collecting plastic bags	99
Summary	100
11. ITALY	103
Chess	104
Mosaics	105
Hand gestures	107
Art and sculpture appreciation	109
Opera	110
Summary	111
12. DENMARK	113
Runes	114
Lego	116
Random acts of kindness	117
Fairy tales	119
Summary	120
13. CHINA	121
Feng Shui	122
Indoor waterfalls	124
Your family tree	126
Papermaking	127
Calligraphy	128
Tai Chi	130
Summary	131

14. THE NETHERLANDS — 133
    Ice Skating — 134
    Cheesemaking — 136
    Flower growing and arranging — 138
    Summary — 139

15. BRAZIL — 141
    Carnaval do Brasil — 142
    Samba — 143
    Cheese bread making — 144
    Armchair caving — 146
    Summary — 148

16. PORTUGAL — 151
    Fandango and Fado — 152
    Bobbin lace-making — 154
    Embroidery — 155
    Canoeing and Kayaking — 156
    Paintball — 157
    Summary — 157

17. FIJI — 159
    Nature trails and Guided Walks — 160
    Lovo – Cooking underground — 161
    Cricket — 163
    Summary — 164

18. THE GAMBIA — 165
    Wood carving — 166
    Drumming — 167
    Summary — 169

19. AUSTRALIA — 171
    Rock art and pebble painting — 172
    Watercolors — 174
    Croquet — 176
    Local history — 177
    Summary — 178

20. LATVIA	181
Mushroom foraging	182
Weaving	184
Dainas	186
Pottery	187
Summary	189
21. JAPAN	191
Ikigai	192
Hanami	192
Kintsugi	194
Kyudo	195
Origami	197
The Haiku	198
Onsen	199
Summary	200
22. THE UNIVERSAL HOBBY	203
Final Thoughts	207
Index	209
References	215
Image Credits	219

101 MORE WAYS TO ENJOY RETIREMENT

Introduction	229
1. INDIA	233
Kite Flying	234
Indian Curry Making	236
Mandala Drawing	239
Design and Mood Board Creation	240
Summary	242
2. SWEDEN	243
Lagom	244
Coffee Culture in Sweden	245
Lördagsgodis	246

Swedish Sauna	247
Döstädning	248
Summary	249
3. IRELAND (ÉIRE)	**251**
Irish Fairies and Leprechauns	252
Watercolor Painting	253
Soda Bread Baking	254
Irish Comedy	256
Duck Herding	257
Summary	259
4. MONGOLIA	**261**
Wire Puzzle Games	262
Ankle Bone Games	263
Build Your Own Yurt	264
Archery	265
Dembee	266
Summary	267
5. SOUTH KOREA	**269**
Hiking	270
Folk Music	271
Fencing	272
Foreign Language Learning	273
Summary	275
6. TURKEY	**277**
Cats and Turks	278
Backgammon	279
Rummikub or Okey	280
Olive Oil Soap Making	281
Tea & Coffee – Turkish style	282
Summary	283
7. OMAN	**285**
Wadi Fun – Riverbed Hiking and Swimming	286
Souk Market Exploration	287
Silversmithing	288

Halawet Ahmad Dessert Making	289
Basket Weaving	290
Summary	291
8. SCOTLAND	293
The Hobby	294
Burns Night	294
The Highland Fling	296
Gurning	297
Home Beer Brewing	298
Summary	299
9. CHILE	301
Chilean Music	302
Flags and their Stories	303
Chilean Ice Cream (and Other Desserts)	304
Poetry Composing	305
UFO Hunting	306
Summary	308
10. CROATIA	309
Christmas Markets	309
Puppetry	311
Water Polo or Swimming	312
Croatian Palačinke Crepes	312
Photography	314
Summary	314
11. ICELAND	317
Genealogy	318
Patterns in Knitting	319
Fermented Shark	320
Sauces in Iceland	321
Tiny Horses	322
Summary	324
12. NEPAL	325
Picnics Nepal Style	326
Acrylic Fluid Mountain Art	327

Felting	328
Singing Bowls	329
Summary	330
13. JAMAICA	**333**
Pirates and Their History	334
Golf	334
Jerk Sauce and Ackee & Saltfish	335
Reggae	336
Summary	337
14. ESTONIA	**339**
Singing	340
Medieval Towns	341
Museum Visits	342
Cross-Country Skiing	343
The Internet	344
Summary	345
15. SOUTH AFRICA	**347**
Online Courses	348
Crossword Creation	348
Jukskei	349
Malva Pudding	350
Crocheting	352
Summary	353
16. SAMOA	**355**
Samoan Umu Cooking	356
'Ie Tōga	357
Samoan Cake Decorating	358
Kilikiti	359
Summary	361
17. LIECHTENSTEIN	**363**
Clog Carving	364
Ribel	364
Stamp Collecting	366

	Macro Photography	367
	Summary	368
18.	EGYPT	369
	Amateur Archaeology	369
	Papyrus Papermaking	370
	Hieroglyphics	372
	Coptic Book-Binding	374
	Senet	375
	Summary	376
19.	ZIMBABWE	377
	Mbira Instrumental Music	378
	Beadwork	379
	Basketry	380
	Muboora Une Dovi Traditional Dish	381
	Shona Sculptures	382
	Summary	384
20.	MEXICO	385
	Jarabe Tapatío Dance	385
	Mexican Yarn Art	387
	Worry Dolls	388
	Mexican Masks	389
	Scratch Art	391
	Tree of Life	392
	Summary	393
21.	PHILIPPINES	395
	Karaoke	396
	Picnics in the Park	397
	Malling	398
	Basketball	399
	Social Media	400
	Summary	401
22.	THE UNIVERSAL HOBBY	403
	Final Thoughts	405
	Image Credits	413

A SPECIAL GIFT JUST FOR YOU!

In '**4 Simple Steps to Create Your Perfect Morning Routine,**' you will discover:

- What a **morning routine** is and why it is essential you have one
- Why having a morning routine will bring you **more focus, productivity, and purpose to your life**
- The secret of creating a morning routine using these **four components** that will **align with your core values**
- How a morning routine can elevate your life so that you may live **vibrantly**, whether you are seeking a companion, exploring new interests, or improving your health

Go to www.ravinachandra.com/books to get it NOW

101 WAYS TO ENJOY RETIREMENT

INTRODUCTION

Your golden years! A chance to explore the world and try out new hobbies – or a chance to take up residence on the couch and do nothing at all?

As we grow older, our bodies tend to slow down, and we become less nimble, less flexible, and less sturdy than in our working years. But it's not all downhill.

Our brains often stay active and alert; however, we may need a little stimulation to encourage us to find the most satisfying ways to spend our leisure time.

When Harry retired, he decided that after his many years of hard physical labor, he would put his feet up and rest. And that is what he did.

He got up about midday – missing the fine mornings and fresh air. Instead, he collapsed onto the couch and stayed there in the dark all afternoon, watching reruns of tv shows he had seen years before. In the evenings, he would stir himself enough to go to the pub and drink too much.

Gradually his friends stopped visiting, even the regulars in the pub began to ignore him, and he found himself very much alone. He almost wished he was back at work.

If only – the saddest words in the English language – if only Harry had found some engaging hobbies to transform his life – if only…

Retirees from all over the world have found interests, stimulation, and exciting things to do and learn about. As you peruse the pages of this book, you will find some hobbies that are familiar to you and some you may have never heard of.

Certain hobbies might need a tweak to adapt them to your own circumstances should you decide to give it a go. For other hobbies, you will at least learn fascinating facts and a multitude of topics for you to consider. I might even go as far as saying, your travel bug within might start planning and packing its bags for your next adventure!

Some activities you can do by yourself; others lend themselves to a group, and many work both ways.

On your journey around the world, as you read this book, you will pick up some hobbies that you can start today which will also keep you evergreen, if I can compare you to a plant! You will visit countries, perhaps some you've previously traveled to, and some places entirely new to you. Either way, it will be a delight to see what other retirees around the world get up to in their spare time. Hopefully, you will be inspired to take up a thing or two yourself!

I have been in healthcare my entire career, and many of my clients are older adults – such a captivating age group. In general, they are engaging, thought-provoking, and some rather inspirational. I know the difficulties age can sometimes bring, but I also know the rewards and wisdom we can gain.

So, open your mind to new experiences and start your journey into the world of 101 hobbies. As a retiree myself, although I left behind my full-time job, I have kept myself engaged by teaching and mentoring older adults part-time, to live their best lives. This includes challenging their brains, keeping curious, and being open to learning new things.

One more thing to mention before you delve into the pages of this book, as I know some of you are wondering why your country is missing.

For every chapter of this book, thorough research and interviews took place to ensure proper representation of hobbies and countries. If you would like your country or hobby featured in upcoming books, I would love to hear from you. A special shout out to my American friends. What a vast and diverse country you have. So stay tuned for your own, special edition of 101 hobbies from across the USA.

Please contact me with your ideas at
ravina@ravinachandra.com

UNITED KINGDOM

What do people find to do on this small, damp, and crowded island?

Well, nowhere is far from the sea! The furthest you can get is the center of England, but no one seems to agree precisely where that is! Lichfield in Staffordshire has a plaque stating it holds the record of 84 miles – and note that the UK still uses miles (1 mile = 1.61 km).

The town of Haltwhistle in Northumberland has banners stating that this is the "Centre of Britain." Meriden near Coventry was known as the center of England since 1829, but this was found to be inaccurate when an attempt to validate this claim was made in 1920.

VISITS TO THE SEASIDE

This universal closeness to the coast means that visits to the seaside are popular, and they suit any age group. You can find almost deserted and stunning cliff-top paths; some are long distances which can take several days to complete, with camping or B&Bs on the way.

But for many, it's simply a day's outing, fish and chips by the sea, ice cream, and other seafood delicacies. Or maybe the trip is just a chance to walk the dog at the local beach.

Note that in some places and at some times of year (even in July), you will go to the beach wearing wellies and macs – and still have a great time buffeting the wind, hearing the screaming seagulls, and braving the icy blast, because...

...there is the pub to warm up in, have a pub lunch, chat with the locals, and learn the latest gossip. Oh, and for those who are confused, wellies and macs are just rubber boots and raincoats.

DRINKING, BRITISH STYLE

Now, talking about locals, when a Brit says "down to the local," they mean the pub.

Pubs in the UK are as unique and different in their clientele as they are in their architecture and atmosphere. There are pubs that are literally hundreds of years old; others are modern, sophisticated metal and glass palaces; but they are all places to meet, drink (another favorite British pastime), and catch up with the latest.

If you visit Britain, a trip to your 'local' will add color and flavor to your visit.

What else do the British find to do in Britain?

TEA DRINKING

In the old days, say fifty years ago, an "afternoon tea" was a feature of English life. You would have strong brown tea, brewed in the pot, then served with milk (always pour the milk in last!) and with it you'd enjoy small sandwiches and – if you were lucky – a piece of Madeira cake.

This has generally been superseded by a mug for every occasion. It is an essential aid for the workmen, the all-important comforter in times of grief or stress. A "cuppa" is still the first line of help in everyday life.

And tea goes further with the increasing consumption of herbal teas, amongst which is chamomile tea. The ritual of making a warm cup of chamomile tea just before bedtime is said to help you get off to sleep gently and easily.

Serve your guests with a tea of your choice, in a pretty teapot, with a stunning home-knitted tea cozy to keep it warm! (An elephant design springs to mind – the trunk over the spout?) This would cement any friendship, and if they reciprocated, you would have a nice little club going with the possibility of meeting new, interesting people.

GO ON A HISTORICAL OUTING

The National Trust and English Heritage are organizations that look after beautiful, rare, and historical sites throughout Britain, and Northern Ireland has a Heritage Trust Network as well. This means that everyone can enjoy a day visiting ancient monuments, lovely gardens, and historic, grand mansions.

If ancient ruins and castles are your main interest, then the heritage sites give a better choice, but the National Trust is the best option for stately homes and gardens. The Scottish Heritage and Welsh Heritage sites allow reduced rates for English Heritage club members.

Wherever you live, there will be fascinating places to visit.

FINE DINING

One popular pastime for mature people is "fine dining clubs." Not only do you get to enjoy a culinary delight, a stay in a nice hotel – often in magnificent surroundings and with pleasant gardens – but it is also the perfect opportunity to meet like-minded people, to engage in intelligent conversation, or even to meet a new partner over candlelight, for long-term friendship or romance.

These dinner parties are suitable for singles as well as couples – and the myths about English food being inedible are simply not true!

Maybe there is a similar club near you? If not, why not start one with a few close friends?

SIGHTSEEING AND PHOTOGRAPHY

Of course, the magnificent scenery is a huge bonus. Scotland and Wales both offer mountains, but these locations are often relatively isolated, so you need to know what you are doing. The saying *"Hope for the best, but prepare for the worst"* is very applicable to venturing into the hills.

The weather is a significant factor in mountain safety: things can change very rapidly in the lonely mountains – even in the lower fells of the beautiful Lake District, England – and the mountain rescue teams, made up of volunteers, are often at full stretch when the clouds descend, and the weather is foul.

As for Northern Ireland, it has to be one of the loveliest countries in the world. If you can, a short visit is accessible from the mainland and will delight your memory bank for years.

Photography is a beautiful hobby for all ages and can enhance memories on cold winter evenings while sharing your experiences with family, friends, and others. You can file photos on your computer and make a lasting folder full of happy memories. First, use the best shots as screen savers to make you smile as they appear on screen. Then, share them with your family – they make a great conversation starter.

TAKE A FURTHER EDUCATION COURSE

England is blessed with many courses at reasonable costs. Universities, old and new, colleges and schools all offer a wide choice of further education courses. Sometimes they are held in beautiful, ancient buildings with stunning grounds. The courses are a rich source of interest as well as friendships and socializing for all ages – and once you have retired, there is no pressure to pass exams! So, get your local leaflet from the library and jump in.

SPEAKERS' CLUBS

English is the language of England and also the primary language spoken in Scotland, Wales, and Northern Ireland. However, those countries also have their own languages: Scottish Gaelic, Welsh, and Irish Gaelic, respectively. So, it's not unnatural that speakers' clubs have developed to promote the use of spoken language.

There are two main speaking organizations in the UK, the International Toastmasters, with its headquarters in the United States, and the Speakers Association, which is UK based.

Both organizations promote excellent speaking skills – and in both, the meetings take on a similar format. Prepared speeches are presented, and an evaluator gives friendly guidance, praising the good points and encouraging improvements. Timing is important, and a traffic light system helps the speaker adjust their speeches to the required length. A topic session, where off-the-cuff short speeches are given, often follows a short break, and a business session might end the meeting.

New members are always welcomed. You can join just for fun, or you can follow the educational pathway the association's structure can provide. You might even go on to participate in competitions at national or international level, but many members just find the interesting topics and friendships made enough reason to join.

So, if there is a club near you – why not give it a go? It can be a tremendous boost to your self-confidence.

SUMMARY

Little "Great Britain" is packed full of beautiful places to see, every step you take is on historic ground – and the weather isn't quite as bad as people often say.

Visit the seaside for a day's outing, which might mean beachcombing, fish and chips, ice cream, or walking. Then, head down to the local (pub) – a great place to meet up, catch up, have a drink, and socialize.

Start a tea-drinking club. Visit heritage sites, and perhaps join a heritage organization. Try fine dining clubs, where you can enjoy culinary delights, meet like-minded people, have intelligent conversation, make new friends, or start long-term relationships.

Enjoy beautiful scenery by sightseeing the beautiful countryside. Indulge in a good camera and try your hand at photography.

Be a lifelong learner: take a course at a renowned institution – several offer online learning, which might suit you wherever you live. Or you could join a speakers' club.

> Day trips to the sea
> Drinking, British style
> Tea drinking
> Go on a historical outing
> Fine dining clubs
> Sightseeing and photography
> Take an educational course
> Speakers' club

THAILAND

Thailand offers lovely scenery, beautiful beaches, and charming people. Sea sports, swimming, scuba diving, and kite surfing are all available in Thailand. Indeed, there is the exuberant nightclub life in the tourist cities, and Thai food is world-renowned for its delicious and delicate flavors.

But there are also reflective activities where calmness and focus on the present moment are given the time necessary for us all to lead a full yet pleasant life.

Thailand has so much to offer, so let's have a look.

SOAP CARVING

Have you ever tried to whittle a piece of wood, hoping to create a recognizable cat or elephant or anything else? If you have, you will know how difficult it can be to get the results you imagined, unless you have a lot of luck or a great deal of talent.

But a solution is at hand! Thailand is famous for its beautiful and elaborate soap carvings. These carvings are something quite special, but with a bit of patience, some practice, and the right tools, you could produce your own masterpiece.

But first, let us look at how soap carving came to Thailand. In the 13th century, Sukhothai had been the historic capital of the Thai Empire for nearly 150 years. People used to carve fruit and vegetables, but it all changed when a king's servant wanted to make her decorations for the Loi Krathong festival stand out. During the festival, decorated baskets were floated on the river. This unnamed servant carved a flower and a bird out of soap to brighten up her basket. And a tradition was born.

Children are often taught soap carving in school, but the real experts produce amazing, fantastical, and elaborate works.

The most common objects carved are traditional flowers and dragons, all in incredible detail.

So how do you start to make your own incredible carving? The steps are as follows:

- Find a soft, inexpensive soap for your first attempts! Rectangular soaps are easier to control than round ones.
- Collect together cutting instruments. These can include a small, sharp knife, a toothpick, and even forks and spoons.
- Lay newspaper underneath your work area to collect up the scraps, which you can remold into usable soap.
- Get rid of the manufacturer's mark by scraping it off under running water, making the soap soft and easier to work.
- Make your design and etch it onto the soap – a toothpick works well.
- Scrape away the outer parts to get the rough outline and then pay attention to the detail.
- Finally, gently polish the soap using your fingers or a paper towel.

And there you have it – a perfect gift for your favorite person. Once you become more skilled, why not use scented soaps, different colors, and of course, nice packaging for a beautiful gift, lovingly made?

YOGA

Yoga is a worldwide phenomenon and extremely popular in Thailand, and many people take up this hobby and give it the respect and practice it deserves. And what better place to practice yoga than on a sandy beach with the sea gently lapping at the shore? Thailand offers its share of lovely landscapes, calm waters, and hilly getaways. Some temples add a sense of serene reflection to yoga, and there are many retreats and workshops, perhaps including meditation, which allies itself so well with yoga.

Thai practitioners have a unique "SomaVeda" way of yoga, combining spiritual and religious additions from ancient practices, incorporating traditional Thai and Chinese medicine, and also including modern science and medicine.

Thailand has a vibrant yoga community and highly skilled teachers, and places to practice with stunning views.

You can do yoga almost anywhere. However, if you intend to take up this as a hobby, you might also like to create a tranquil place in your own home where you can peacefully get into a calm state and focus on getting the best out of your yoga. Many now do yoga by watching instructions online. But there are likely yoga classes to attend in your vicinity, too.

You may also decide that a weekend yoga retreat, such as they have in Thailand, would be a superb way to start, and meeting like-minded people is one of the benefits of such a retreat. This would be a wonderful way to get away, treating your mind and body well.

Yoga is far more than just exercise. It strengthens and stretches your muscles, making them supple and flexible while creating a space for calm reflection and mental healing.

And it is harder than it looks!

COLLECTING AMULETS

This unusual hobby is popular in Thailand. There are huge markets devoted just to amulets, and department stores may have an entire floor just for them.

Thailand has a Buddhist majority, so collecting religious objects is something many Thai people like to do. And the value of these objects can rise into thousands of dollars if a well-respected monk blesses them.

Many collectors are proud to show their friends their delightful objects, although one of the most successful collectors keeps his collection well hidden in velvet-lined boxes in a vault. They are treated with respect, for they are valuable and beautiful.

Amulets might be very ancient and show the marks of time. Some may be embellished with jewels and the glitter of gold. Amulet collections are full of mystery. Who owned them? Where do they come from? Are they ancient artifacts, or were they made just down the road?

Many retirees collect things; it is just something people do. As children, we collect shells and rocks, and maybe Pokémon cards. Sometimes we continue to collect as adults: stamp collecting, for example, is a worldwide and interesting hobby. Coins and comic books are other potentially valuable and interesting collections. Other people collect such things as "do not disturb" signs, spoons, water pistols, and knitting patterns.

When you start collecting stamps, perhaps you may be delving into the history, finding fascinating facts about your past, and even building up a valuable asset to pass on to your children. People may travel the world to find that rare stamp or that extraordinary coin. So it may be worth looking over your childhood collections; just maybe you will find an 1840 Victorian "penny black" from England – the first stamp ever produced.

If comics are your interest, keep them in mint condition to hold their value, just as the amulet collectors in Thailand keep their beautiful collections.

There is an infinite number of things one can collect, and the amulets of Thailand are just one example of a relatively unusual and interesting collection.

SCUBA DIVING

You may already go down to the sea with a snorkel and flippers. Even with just these items, you can see so much hidden from the surface view, but if you want to delve deeper, then Thailand is a perfect place to learn how to do it – the safe and proper way.

Thailand offers some of the best scuba diving in the world. With the warm seas, shallow areas near beaches, and safe diving sites, it is not surprising that scuba diving in Thailand is famous, and many Thai divers are very skilled.

This is a sport that needs proper training and equipment. The island of Koh Tao offers courses for people to reach the Professional Association of Diving Instructors (PADI) certification, and there are just so many beautiful places for a beginner to explore.

I should emphasize that we are not talking about cave diving, which is one of the most dangerous sports in the world, as was demonstrated in 2018 when a boys soccer team and their coach were stranded in a deep cave that was flooding. The fast-approaching monsoon added dangerously to the water levels. The best cave divers from Britain, Australia, the US, and China, plus the superb Thai navy seals, managed to rescue them ten days after they went missing, in an epic rescue operation, which claimed the life of one of the rescuers.

Instead, we are talking about diving at a gentle pace after training and preferably in warm seas under optimum conditions for a new look at what is under the waves. Scuba diving is addictive, and you need to be reasonably healthy to be safe.

But even with just your snorkel and flippers, you can add value to your dip in the sea – you never know what you may find!

THAI COOKING

One cannot leave Thailand without sampling its cuisine, and there are many online courses available to teach you, step by step, to make some fantastic meals to astonish your friends and family.

Thai food reflects the history of Thailand. Many years ago, people from southern China emigrated to Thailand, bringing their culinary influence. In olden times, the Buddhist religion determined their choice of food. They ate a mainly plant-based diet with the addition of seafood. Meat was only eaten in small quantities – strips of meat were flavored with spices and herbs or shredded after cooking.

It was the Portuguese missionaries who first brought spices to Thailand in the late 1600s. A lady called Maria Guyomar de Pinha influenced Thai cooking. She was of mixed Japanese Portuguese-Bengali descent and married Constantine Phaulkon, a Greek adviser to King Narai.

So Thai menus owe much to their global origins, and they appeal to many people around the world today. Despite these complex origins, Thai cuisine does not have to be fearfully elaborate, and you can produce delightful meals quite easily if you know how. Add a few candles and flowers for a perfect or romantic night at home with people you care about.

If you consider yourself a foodie, like my husband and I do, then having a hobby of adventuresome cooking might be right up your alley. You could start with one type of food like Thai and build your repertoire as you circle the globe. I am sure your friends and family won't mind being your taste testing group.

SUMMARY

Thailand is a beautiful country with some beautiful hobbies. Carving with soap, you can create unique and lovely items without the physical pressure needed for carving with wood.

Adventuring under the sea is just as fascinating as exploring on land, and scuba diving in Thailand seems the natural thing to do. Courses are available at most beach resorts, so you can go scuba diving safely and explore the best underwater places.

All around the world, people are doing yoga, and Thailand has some scenic places to get out your mat and do a spot of yoga. So many people benefit from the controlled movements and serene mindset; it seems a shame not to try it yourself.

Collecting amulets is rather special: amulets are historically intriguing as well as often very beautiful. But people collect just about everything, from acorns to rare stamps. Maybe you can find something collectible that stirs your interest?

Who hasn't eaten Thai cooking? It's a favorite with many people, and if you can cook up a delicious Thai menu, your guests will be impressed. But why wait till you have visitors?

      Soap carving
      Yoga
      Amulet collecting
      Scuba diving
      Thai cookery

BELGIUM

As you may know already, Belgium is famed for its chocolate, sausages, and beer.

HOT-AIR BALLOONING

Are you surprised to see hot-air ballooning is popular in Belgium? The Belgian Balloon Trophy is an annual event attracting competitors from far away. The air is filled with colorful balloons drifting across the sky; it's balloon festival time!

And many other times, when you are walking in the forests, driving along the splendid motorways, or hurrying along the pavements in town, you may look up and catch a glimpse of a balloon sailing by, high above in a clear blue sky.

A balloon ride

Many companies arrange balloon rides during the summer months, and it's exciting to anticipate what the ride will feel like if you've never been up in a hot air balloon.

Surprisingly, you often need to get up very early in the morning since the air in the balloon must be hotter than the outside air. The outside air has to be stable as well, and during the day, the atmosphere heats up and creates thermals that destabilize the air.

You arrive on site in the half-light of early dawn. You find the balloon on the ground, tethered and tugging at the ropes. A fire has been lit beneath the canopy; the air heats up, the balloon pulls harder – it's time to get in the basket.

You climb over the sides of the wicker basket; you can feel it jumping around a little as the balloon seems impatient to start the ascent.

The ropes are released, and you start to rise.

You can hear the flames of the fire heating the air; you can feel a breeze. It's still early, and the air outside is cool. You gaze over the side as the ground recedes; soon, you are floating gently over the landscape, over the fields, above the treetops.

You can see the shadow of the balloon on the ground below, keeping track with you. Maybe you pass over a farmyard and set the dogs barking. Perhaps you are sailing over the top of a town and can see the tiny cars below you. It all seems far away – all your cares are distant. For a brief while, life flows naturally around you. It's exhilarating and calm at the same time.

All too soon, the journey is over, and you arrive back at the start field and land with a bump.

Mind you, you don't always land exactly where you set off! The balloon is at the mercy of the wind, and steering can be almost non-existent.

How high you fly will depend on local regulations, but most will reach around 3,000 feet. The wicker baskets contain between two and eleven passengers and are designed to be light and slightly flexible. Hot-air ballooning is the safest form of air travel, so apart from the bump as you land, your journey should be smooth and comfortable.

You will need to research whether there is a hot air balloon club available where you live. If not a full-time hobby, it is certainly worth investigating as a fun outing, at home or on your next visit to Belgium.

GHOST HUNTING IN BELGIUM

Belgium has no shortage of abandoned buildings and haunts for ghosts. So, let's look at a few of them:

The Abandoned Castle – Miranda Château

This is a lovely building, falling into decay. Originally built by French émigrés fleeing the guillotine, this would be a haven for ghosts.

Unfortunately, this building has been neglected since 1991 and is now threatened with demolition. But it is the perfect place for ghost hunters.

Haunted House in Sas-van-Gent

This haunted house was famous and, in its heyday, attracted ghost hunters from all over Europe.

Local legend has it that a German soldier was electrocuted nearby, and his ghost haunts the house. Four Canadian soldiers joined him when a mine in WWII destroyed their tank.

This house has now become something of a legend. Rumor has it that doors slammed, cameras misted up, watches stopped, and cell phones became inactive when ghost hunters visited this haunted house. But now, we'll never know since the house was demolished in 2011 for health and safety reasons.

The John McCrae Bunker

In WWI, John McCrae wrote a famous poem that starts like this:

In Flanders fields the poppies blow
Between the crosses, row on row,
That mark our place; and in the sky
The larks, still bravely singing, fly
Scarce heard amid the guns below.

We are the Dead. Short days ago
We lived, felt dawn, saw sunset glow,
Loved and were loved, and now we lie,
In Flanders fields.

In 1918, he died while looking after wounded comrades. The bunker where he was working has become a WWI memorial site and is said to be haunted by his ghost. Visitors have heard the echoes of gunshots – and some even claim to have seen the ghost of Alexis Helmer, to whom this poem was dedicated.

The Lady of La Roche

Once upon a time, there lived a nobleman in the castle of la Roche. He had a very beautiful daughter called Berthe.

He decided to hold a tournament for the lady's hand in marriage. Among the competitors was Count of Montaigu, although he was already engaged to another lady, Countess Alix de Salm. He seemed to be winning every joust – until the very end when a small knight in black armor killed him and took Berthe to the bridal chamber.

The following morning, Berthe and the black knight were found dead at the foot of the cliffs below the chamber's window.

The black knight was discovered to be Countess Alix de Salm. She had made a pact with the devil. She wanted to kill her cheating fiancé and the lady who was to become his wife. And now, her ghost haunts the castle.

The castle hosts ghost events, parties, and fireworks – and these events are very impressive.

Bruges' Legendary Haunted House

In 1498, there was a nunnery in Bruge and a monastery on the opposite side of the river. It had to happen – a young monk fell in love with Hortense, one of the nuns. He found a secret under-the-river tunnel and paid her visits, but Hortense rejected him and tried to escape his clutches. In a rage, the monk stabbed her to death and buried her. Now both their ghosts are said to haunt the area – Hortense clothed in white and the monk seeking her to beg forgiveness – but he can never find her, and at midnight, both ghosts disappear.

GARAGE SALES

In Belgium, they do things on a grand scale. These are not just your typical little garage sales: the whole village turns out their belongings for sale in their front gardens, in their driveways, and on the pavement. The police put out warning notices, and homemade adverts litter the highways for days ahead.

From fresh garden produce to antique butter dishes, books, and toast racks, you can find almost anything. In addition, these sales can be a great source of old but valuable vinyl records and CDs if you know what you are looking for. Even children's furniture and toys are bargains to be snatched up. These mini markets are also a friendly social gathering and a wonderful place to catch up on the local comings and goings.

Garage saling, yard sale shopping, or flea markets as they call it can be popular all around the world. If this is something that appeals to you, definitely check out what's happening in your own community. After attending a few yourself, you might find that you are hooked and make this a weekly occurrence, both to sell stuff and acquire new finds!

PATCHWORK FANTASIES

Patchwork is a global hobby, and Belgium has its share of skilled needlewomen. These skilled hobbyists can produce unique patchwork goods, an absolute joy to see.

While patchwork is a hobby that can be enjoyed alone, it is also a relaxing way to meet like-minded men and women. Groups meet in after-school classrooms, church rooms, and other venues. Typically, with these types of clubs, there will be a break with soup, tea, or coffee and a selection of savory and sweet snacks to keep up your energy.

The conversation will be what any group of people typically talk about – spouses, children, schools, pets, weather, and health, together with the latest local gossip.

So busy are the women and men chatting away; it's almost magical how they produce such beautiful things.

Every few weeks, huge markets devoted solely to materials for sewing are set up – a focus for people from miles around to snatch up bargain fabrics of every kind imaginable. It makes an enjoyable day out as you meander your way home with bags full of promise.

One of the best ways to get supplies for patchwork is to use up scraps of material from past clothes. You can make a family quilt that reminds you of the pretty dress your granddaughter loved or the shirt your husband wore and wore until it was almost threadbare, and you finally managed to sneak it out of the closet.

Patchwork can be used to make bags and sacs and covers for boxes and books. You might also make covers for your pouf or chair and oven gloves to protect your hands. Of course, they can simply be decorative, and some of the finest examples are hangings to adorn your walls.

A patchwork gift shows thoughtfulness and care, so it is always a pleasing gift to receive. Matching and mixing the different materials is creative and results in unique articles made with love! If you have at least one creative bone in your body, patchwork might be your next new hobby!

JIGSAWS

Jigsaws are popular wherever you go. They are one way to create an amazing picture but also a way to learn about places, animals, and birds, etc. A jigsaw of an old master (famous painting) is a fun way to study art; you really can see the details of the painting when you have to put it together piece by piece.

Belgium has jigsaw groups and competitions. Individuals, pairs, or teams compete to complete a 500 or 5000-piece jigsaw, and it might take several hours. This is an excellent way to make friends, and the competing element makes it quite exciting as competing teams near the end of the competition.

How does the last piece fit?

There is a wide assortment of jigsaws in Belgium; there's even one of the Belgian flag. It's a great way to learn your way around places you may want to visit – or places you never will. You won't get lost in Bruges if you have already completed a jigsaw of a map of the city!

There is not only a vast range of jigsaws but there are also a variety of ways to store the unfinished piece without demolishing it. Framing and hanging your special puzzle is a great way to have continued enjoyment.

Why not ask your friends to join in and either complete a jigsaw together or compete to see who can finish a similar one first? Last year I joined an enjoyable Facebook group dedicated to the art of puzzling, and I competed (it was a very friendly competition) in a jigsaw jamboree over a three-month period where each participant had to complete as many 1500 piece or more puzzles in the allotted 90 days. There were weekly prizes and giveaways, and even my husband joined in the fun. I plan to participate again this upcoming year.

SUMMARY

This small country with its energetic and stoic people is full of ideas to amuse you.

The castles and ghosts, together with the pretty scenery in the Ardennes, offer many exciting outings, and for the evenings, there are patchwork groups and jigsaws to keep you entertained.

When you want to clear the clutter, why not have a garage sale? You might even make some money, which you could put towards an extraordinary trip – a balloon ride! There is truly nothing like it for putting things into perspective and seeing the world from a small distance – a marvelous way to clear your mind and enjoy a few moments of serenity.

>Hot-air ballooning
>Ghost hunting
>Garage sales
>Patchwork
>Jigsaw puzzles

FRANCE – L'HEXAGONE

When we think of France, we think of chic, fashion, that peculiarly Gallic sense of independent thinking, and wonderful wines. The French are justifiably proud of their beautiful country and have found a unique way to showcase it with the Tour de France.

Every region has its own specialty. Champagne is only from the Champagne region (whatever any other labels may say). Another example is the Roquefort classic blue cheese made from ewe's milk from Roquefort. Both names are protected by law – at least in France.

The scenery varies from the pink flamingos in the salty marshes in the south, where over 60,000 flamingos migrate, to the sophisticated, sunny beaches of Cannes and Nice, where the luxury yachts dock. Then there are the old hunting forests of the kings and the highest mountain in the Alps, Mont Blanc.

So, let's take a tour with the Tour de France, which visits many areas of "l'Hexagone," as the French people like to call their country.

THE TOUR DE FRANCE

The Tour de France is an incredibly arduous race. It all started in 1903 when two sports newspapers, *Le Vélo* and *L'Auto*, were in competition. L'Auto formed after disagreements between journalists about the "Dreyfus affair," which resulted in the execution of an innocent man for treason and divided France at the time.

The race was intended to boost the circulation of the new paper "L'Auto," whose editor was a keen cyclist. While bicycle races were a common type of newspaper promotion at the time, the massive scale of this race was intended to put Le Vélo out of business.

The race has undergone many changes since its inception. Now it is a multi-stage race, and the winner of each stage is entitled to wear the prestigious yellow jersey for the next stage. Each stage lasts a day, and there are 21 stages over 23 days, usually taking place in early July when the sun beats down fiercely.

Historically, the person placed last had a red lantern attached to the rear of their bike! (This attracted sympathy – and a bigger check!)

Every year the route changes to showcase a new area of l'Hexagone. But the mountainous Pyrenees and Alps are always included, together with the finishing line on the Champs-Élysées in Paris.

The tour is grueling. In 1903, many riders dropped out in the first race – it was too exhausting – leaving only 24 competitors at the end of the fourth stage. During its history, infighting, underhanded tactics, and drugs have all played a part. Four deaths have occurred; one rider drowned in a river during a rest break.

So, bicycle riding is immensely popular in France, where cycling seems to be a national hobby for all ages and all fitness levels. You see kids on bikes, women with baskets of flowers or shopping, as well as young men and the older generation, all enjoying the thrill of the wind in their faces and the lovely scenery they explore. This hobby could start at any age, even if you didn't do a lot of bike riding as a child.

More and more city planners within communities are dedicated to creating bike lanes and bike-only paths throughout their cities and natural surroundings, so pick up the latest cycling pamphlet if you are intrigued with getting on a bicycle again. It seems a trend of the past few years is electric bikes, which help on longer adventures. I've even seen three-wheeler types which would be very stable if you have balance issues; it looks like these modern tricycles may be the latest trend.

BOULES OR PÉTANQUE

Another French sport is a little less arduous. Wherever you go in France, you will find people playing boules. As you enter a village there will be a group, usually of men, playing boules on a patch of land. It doesn't matter if the ground is uneven; it doesn't matter if there are tree stumps in the way; the game can still be played. But, of course, the older players have the advantage of familiarity with the terrain! There are also "boulodromes" dedicated to the sport with gravel or hard dirt surfaces.

The game is deceptively simple: a small target ball called the jack is thrown down, and with larger balls called boules, players aim to either hit the jack, land close to it or dislodge their opponents' boule. The name is derived from words meaning "foot fixed," so the player must keep his or her feet firmly anchored to the ground while throwing. One can play solo or as a member of a team.

The game itself goes right back to ancient Greece and Egypt. In the sixth century BC, the Greeks tossed coins, then flat stones and later stone balls, attempting to throw them as far as possible. Finally, the Romans added a target, and this variation came to France with the legions.

The balls became wooden, and in England, King Henry III forbade his soldiers from playing boules – they had to practice their archery instead – while in France, the ban on boules extended to commoners – only 300 years later, in the 17th century, was the ban lifted.

Nowadays, technology has improved, and the balls are usually hollow metal boules, which are cheap to mass-produce, and they are now exported to many countries around the world. Every two years, the Fédération Internationale de Pétanque et Jeu Provençal (FIPJP) world championships take place, with the contests alternating between the mens' and the womens' competitions. But still, the best-known competition happens in Marseille, in France, which attracts over 10,000 combatants and 150,00 spectators.

Formal games require teams of one, two, or three players. The players stand in a marked circle to throw the boules; the circles are now prefabricated 50 cm circles of red plastic often used in formal games. The number of boules for each player depends on the number in the team: in singles and doubles, each member has three boules, but in triples, each player has only two.

Points are scored for the team with the closest boule to the little wooden target, now called a "cochonnet"– and once the magic number of 13 is reached, the winning team can be announced.

There is one very odd custom. A "carreau" is a winning shot – it knocks away the opponent's boule and takes its place. But if the team scores no points, it is known as "fanny," and the losing team must kiss the bottom of a girl named "Fanny"!

Fortunately, the team comes prepared – and that explains why you may see an image or small carved figure of a barebottomed girl with the team.

CHAMPAGNE AND CHARTREUSE

Champagne, as we all know, is a sparkling wine that comes from Champagne in France. To gain the appellation "champagne," the grapes must be grown in designated areas, and the grape-pressing must be done in a specific way.

The Romans first planted grapes in the area and red wines were produced in Champagne before medieval times, but the first sparkling white champagne was produced by accident. Bottles exploded, corks flew out, and the wine was known as "the devil's wine!"

It was near the medieval town of Carcassonne that the first record of sparkling wine was made in a Benedictine abbey in

1531. They achieved the sparkling form by bottling the wines before fermentation had been completed.

One hundred years later, an Englishman found that by adding sugar, the wine fermented again, and in 1662, another Englishman found out how to make glass bottles strong enough to resist the bubbles.

Six years later, Dom Pérignon entered the scene with the task of getting rid of the pesky bubbles. The workers had to wear heavy iron masks to protect their faces from bursting bottles, and cellars often lost up to 90% of their bottles by spontaneous bursting! But Dom Pérignon is credited with many innovations needed to produce this world-class wine, revered throughout the world.

Chartreuse

Less well known than champagne are chartreuse liqueurs, produced near Grenoble. Like champagne, the alcohol was created initially by religious communities for the taking of the holy sacrament. However, unlike champagne, chartreuse continues to be a closely guarded secret, only available to two individuals, both monks in the Grande Chartreuse monastery.

The story goes that in 1605, a French marshal of artillery to the French king, Henry IV, gave the Carthusian monks at a monastery near Paris a recipe for the "elixir of long life." So valuable was this that it ended up in the headquarters of the religious order near Grenoble, in the beautiful Chartreuse mountains. The recipe includes about 130 plants, flowers, herbs, and secret ingredients in an alcohol base. And ever since 1737, the monks have made and sold chartreuse.

There followed a somewhat checkered history. The monks were expelled from France in 1793, as were all the other religious orders. Manufacturing ceased. A copy of the recipe was made, but the monk carrying it was arrested and imprisoned in Bordeaux. However, he was able to pass the document to his friend Dom Basile Nantas. This friend believed that the monks would remain in Spain and never return, so he sold the recipe to a pharmacy in Grenoble.

Napoleon ordered that the ministry of the interior must review every recipe for secret medicine. The manuscript was sent and duly returned marked "refused." When the pharmacist died, his heirs sent it back to the monks who had indeed returned to the monastery.

The monks were expelled again in 1903. The monks took their recipe with them to Catalonia and continued to produce their liqueur. But they have now returned to France and produce green and yellow varieties of this quite sweet and spicy tasting chartreuse. And the longer the spirit stays in the bottle, the better it tastes. Today, you can take a tour of the distillery and taste the sweet chartreuse.

Chartreuse is sometimes used as an ingredient in cocktails and was on the menu in a pudding on the Titanic the night it sank. It is another example of a regional drink gaining a worldwide reputation for excellence.

Unsurprisingly in a country so renowned for its wine, tours of wine cellars, weekend wine tasting sessions, and wine-making weekends are very much in evidence. All over France, you can find workshops devoted to winemaking and appreciation, sometimes combined with golf or even ballooning.

In many countries, people can learn about wine, taste the specialties and enjoy wine in their homes. Some people store fine wines or spirits as an investment and can build up a valuable collection. It can be seen as quite a sophisticated hobby. Maybe this is for you?

PERFUME

When it comes to perfume, France is the world leader with 30% of the global market. Some of the most famous names in the industry are French, including Chanel, Christian Dior, and Estée Lauder. Chanel N°5 is perhaps the most iconic fragrance of all time. Famous perfumeries such as the Maison Guerlain are French.

One French perfume – Clive Christian's No. 1 Imperial Majesty – entered the Guinness Book of World Records as the most expensive perfume and was a limited edition presented in diamond-studded Baccarat crystal flagons.

But there is another side to French perfume. The lovely lavender fields of Provence are a riot of purples and lilacs in August. If you walk in the capital of Provence, the town of Sault, you will find everything scented with lavender – even, it is said, the roses!

Lavender has so many uses: it can be added to soaps, scented candles, little sachets to scent your laundry, and of course, lavender bags to place under your pillow to help you sleep. Lavender is also added to flavor honey and ice cream – it's everywhere.

Small lavender bags make cute little presents and are very easy to make. And if your hobby is making candles, why not use lavender to scent them?

BOULEVARD LIFE IN PARIS

What strikes a foreigner in Paris is the number of cafés on the pavements. It's a beautiful place to sip a coffee and watch the world go by – and nearly everyone does it.

These cafés serve as a social meeting place, a place to relax and unwind, and often provide meals any time of day as well as a nice glass of wine.

The French take coffee drinking to a new height. They may ask for a "grande crème" (a large white coffee), the small black espresso, or the anise-flavored "pastis." The larger coffees and hot chocolates are typically served in bowls, making them easier to dunk your croissant in!

You may see the men playing checkers or reading the newspapers. The cafés are a popular place to eat your croissant for breakfast.

The oldest surviving Paris café is the Café Procope, which opened in 1686. Cafés like this didn't always have a good reputation: before the French Revolution, they were seen as "the ordinary refuge of the idler and the shelter of the indigent."

But things have changed. In the hurly-burly of a busy city, these cafés are little oases, offering a chance to sit back, meet friends and see the world passing by. It seems to me that enjoying a coffee at your favorite café, especially if it allows you time to people-watch, read the paper and converse with old friends, would be considered a satisfying life-long hobby most would appreciate.

SUMMARY

France has some stunning scenery, and what better way to showcase it than a long and arduous cycle ride? You don't have to compete in the Tour de France to enjoy a bicycle (or tandem) ride in your local country; it's surprising how far you can go.

Boules is a game anyone can take part in – strategy is everything!

France is justly proud of its wines and its perfumes. You can appreciate wines and even use them as an investment. You may not be able to reproduce the scents of Paris. Still, you could enjoy using lavender to make candles or lavender bags – wonderful gifts, especially for anyone who has trouble getting off to sleep.

Breakfast on the boulevard is a very french thing, but why not emulate them (weather permitting)? It's an excellent, relaxing way to start the day.

>Cycling
>Boules
>Wine appreciation
>Lavender bags or candles
>Breakfast on the boulevard

CANADA

Canada is vast. There is a stunning range of beautiful scenery from the sea and mountains in the west to the Great Lakes and Hudson Bay in the east, and variable, mixed weather: snow and ice, hot sun, and everything in between. And Canadians know how to make the most of it. Exploring their country by camper van is a popular choice for all ages. Curling and pickleball keep Canadians fit, and for the quieter times, nothing beats a good read.

CURLING

Curling started in Scotland in the sixteenth century. Scots played on frozen lochs and ponds. In 1541, the first recorded match was held between a monk from Paisley Abbey and one of the abbot's relatives. It's good to know the monks enjoyed themselves.

But since then, curling has come to Canada in a big way; between eighty and ninety percent of curlers in the world are Canadian! Yet still, the best stones are made from granite, and that granite was traditionally mined only in the Trefor Quarry in Wales or Ailsa Craig – an offshore Scottish island. The world curling championships only permit stones made from the granite of Ailsa Craig (Craig means rock), and there is one company with the exclusive right to harvest Ailsa Craig granite to make curling stones. The world championship in 2021 was held in Calgary (and was won by Sweden).

The stones weigh between thirty-eight and forty-four pounds, including the handle, and a new stone will cost around $450 (USD), although a used one will be considerably cheaper.

Yelling on the sidelines is part of the fun. Sayings like "hurry," "hurry hard," and "clean" all have their own particular meanings. The atmosphere is electric; the stone slides with unbelievable speed, the teams race, and the audience roars.

EXPLORING WITH A CAMPER VAN OR RV

See the country in comfort, and control where and when you stop. What could be better than a camper van?

You get lovely countryside, that back-to-nature feeling, freedom to go where you like, and evenings by the campfire – all without having to erect a tent!

Canada is a free country, and almost ninety percent of the country is designated "Crown land," and usually, you can camp there free for twenty-one days if you are a Canadian citizen. However, you need to be careful not to camp on private land – always ask first!

You can often even park overnight in a shopping mall parking lot.

Since most people stay overnight in designated places, you will find toilets and hot showers, as most camper vans do not have them installed. However, portable toilets are available (though they can be smelly!)

You may prefer an RV (recreational vehicle), which does have all modern conveniences installed. Many retired people become real pros and bring their potted plants, doormats, and even the kitchen sink.

A few tips worth bearing in mind:

- Mosquitoes can be a bane if they like you. Be prepared!
- Bumpy side roads can cause chaos if your belongings are not firmly strapped down.
- Book your campsite ahead in the busy season. The best sites are often the most popular and get full – not what you want after a long day's drive.
- Nights can be chilly, so be sure to take extra layers.
- Take an old-fashioned road map in case you visit locations off signal.

Camper van adventures not only let you visit and absorb different parts of Canada but also often give you a break from your screens and phones. They can be as sociable as you please, as you can spend time outside, mixing with other campers, yet you can also be alone with nature if that is your wish.

My good friend Barb took up camping with her newly acquired camper van just a year or so ago. She recently told me that she had camped 118 nights so far this year! Most places she camps are not that far from home. She just loves retired life, calling herself "one happy camper." If the weather turns for the worse, she can stay snug as a bug inside her tiny camper home.

PICKLEBALL

In the mid-1960s, pickleball was born. Starting as a children's backyard game, it became increasingly popular in community centers, parks, schools, and retirement communities.

The story goes that three friends returned from playing golf and found their families were bored. So they thought of playing badminton, but no one could find the shuttlecock, so they improvised. They lowered the net, found a perforated plastic ball, made paddles from plywood, and took the name from the family cocker spaniel who retrieved the balls – or so rumor has it.

It is estimated that Canada now has around 60,000 players – and no wonder. The game is easy to score and not too challenging to play. It may look like tennis, it may sound like ping-pong, but it is developing into a game in its own right, not unlike badminton. It is ideal for older adults who are keeping fit.

The game is played on a court, which is smaller than a tennis court, so perhaps needs a little less energy expenditure? Players say otherwise! It is usually played as doubles, using small paddles to send the ball over the net.

The aim is to keep the ball low, below waist level, although overarm strokes are sometimes used. Huge tennis smashes are not a prominent feature of pickleball. This game needs a strategy to win, and letting the opponent make the mistakes to gain points is one crafty one! The first to reach the score of eleven is the winning team.

But there is a strange language growing up around pickleball: words like dink, erne, forex, gentleman's rally, kitchen, nasty nelson, out-of-the-jar, poach, and the more familiar lob.

Para-pickleball (played from a wheelchair) is also becoming popular – with similar rules to the parent game. It seems this energetic game requires mental agility as much as physical strength, so it is well suited to seniors.

LITTLE FREE LIBRARIES

These delightful mini-libraries are popping up all over Canada. They consist simply of a waterproof box with a see-through door, stuck on a pillar low enough for a child to reach, with room for just a handful of books. Often these little boxes are painted and nicely decorated.

Wherever you go, be sure to keep your eyes peeled – you can find these delightful boxes on the streets, in parks, along walking trails, and in many other places. Sometimes people gather to chat about the books they have read and advise you on your next read, so they also act as social focal points.

And what better way to encourage youngsters to read as they leave the park with a book in their hand?

You might find a little library in a train or bus station – out of the rain – and this might provide the perfect reading matter for your travels. Community centers and church porches could also be great places for a mini library.

These mini-libraries tend to be set up in moderately high-income areas, so a school counselor, Sarah Kamya from New York, decided to take the idea a step further and developed little free diverse libraries to encourage people to understand life from a different perspective. She bought books by Black and Indigenous authors – and this has taken off in a big way.

She only started in June 2020, but she has already donated thousands of books and raised thousands of dollars, helping to make Black and Indigenous people's voices heard throughout America and Canada.

Starting a little library is not too hard: a box, a pole, and a few books, and you are set up. However, if you have a mission like Sarah Kamya, then you have much more work to do in keeping your library stocked with books to support your mission.

Little Free Diverse Libraries Today

LFDL is now a non-profit organization that aims to spread diverse books through the little libraries. This can inspire deep conversations about some of the issues which face us all. The aim is to expand the number of mini-libraries, especially in places where the need is greatest.

But for anyone wanting a book to read, what could be easier than plucking one out of the mini box? It can be a great pleasure for those who have too many books to pop them in the box and know that someone else will get delight from reading them.

SUMMARY

Canada has such a range of stunning scenery – and such a range of weather as well. Of course, exploring the beautiful scenery by camper van makes sense, but you could also range afar in an RV and see new places in comfort.

Curling and pickleball are both games to play or to watch, and when you feel the need to settle down with a good book, what can be better than having access to a little library, even if you have to make it yourself?

>	Curling
>	Camper van or RV exploration
>	Pickleball
>	Mini libraries

GREECE

P icture Greece, and what do you see? Whitewashed buildings and blue-domed churches? Beaches and islands and ancient ruins? But did you know that

80% of Greece is made up of mountains? Greece is one of the most mountainous countries in Europe.

And the Greeks don't call themselves "Greek"; they prefer the name "Hellene."

Greece has an impressive coastline. In addition to the mainland, the country consists of over 6000 lovely islands, 227 of them inhabited, collectively comprising almost 10,000 miles of coastline with blue seas and stunning views.

With their hot summers and outdoor lifestyle, hobbies tend to be based on the sea or mountains – and yes, you can ski in Greece in the winter, using one of the 117 ski lifts.

You could visit an ancient monument in the morning, laze on the beach all afternoon, and take a stroll up and down the main street with the locals in the evening.

SWIMMING IN THE SEA

There is nothing quite as refreshing as a swim in the sea, and the waters around Greece are pleasantly warm. In the early morning, you might have a little cove all to yourself, and it's a wonderful way to wake up. In the afternoon, a dip in the sea is relief from the hot sun. The dolphin is the national animal for Greece, so if you are lucky, you might see them frolicking around.

The island of Santorini has different colored beaches – red, white, and black – due to the volcanic activity. And you never know what you may find. There are ruins under the waves – cities long awaiting rediscovery – and maybe in the shallow seas near the beaches; you will find echoes of the past. You can even wade out to the ruin of the ancient city of Epidaurus and see a Roman villa, or you could take a kayak. Warm waters, breath-taking glimpses of the past, and a welcoming taverna on the beach – what better way to spend an evening.

One word of warning about sea bathing in Greece – shoes or sturdy sandals will prevent your walk in the water from ending with painful sea urchin spines embedded in your feet!

TAVLI ON THE SIDEWALKS

In Greece, you can't miss the men sitting sipping their ouzo or coffee, playing board games on little tables outside the cafe.

The commonest game is "Tavli" – which is Greek for board. This can be played by families, although it is more typically the men who play.

There are three commonly played games of Tavli: Portes is a little like backgammon, with slightly different rules, Plakoto is more like checkers, and Fevga is another variation on checkers. The games date back thousands of years. So you are never far from ancient history in Greece.

Greeks play the games one after the other, for three, five, or seven Tavli points. The game is played fast, with one dice to be shared and picked up quickly, but if you throw while the opponent is still holding their piece, then you are penalized. It can be quite nail-biting.

This game is addictive. And in the pleasantly cool evenings, what nicer way to spend the evening hours than with friends playing Tavli outside the local cafe in summer.

OLIVE APPRECIATION

For over 6000 years, olives have been grown, harvested, and pressed for oil. The earliest evidence of olive farming is in the eastern Mediterranean countries. Now olives are grown in many countries and on every continent except Antarctica.

Greece is the third-largest producer of olives – about 2.2 million metric tons every year – second only to Spain and Italy, but Greece claims to grow more varieties.

Most of us know there are green and black olives, yet there are actually 139 varieties. Ninety percent of them are pressed for their oil; the other ten percent we see on our tables and decorating our pizzas. All olives start off green and slowly ripen to light brown, reddish-purple, and finally to the deep black we all know.

Like fine wines, olives all have their own unique flavor, which is influenced by the variations in cultivating, harvesting, and processing, even within the same grove.

Olive oils may be produced from a single variety or a blend from two or more different ones. As a result, there is a lot to learn about olives and their oils.

Just to emphasize the importance of olives to Greece, the patron saint of olives is Athena. Why was she chosen over all the other gods? Athena is the goddess of warfare and wisdom. To win the people over, she used her wisdom to give a gift they could not refuse – an olive tree. The Athenians thought this a better gift than that of water offered by Poseidon.

ANCIENT HISTORY & MYTHOLOGY

Greece is the cradle of Western civilization, so museums and ancient ruins are popular places to visit for Hellenes and tourists alike. Greece has over 500 archaeological sites, most of which are open to the public. Greek history is intrinsically linked with the myths of the ancient gods.

Famous sites include the Parthenon in Athens and the Temple of Apollo at Delphi, which was once home to the famous oracle. In the eighth century BCE, pilgrims came from far and wide to ask the Oracle of Delphi, the high priestess known as the Pythia, to foretell their future. Before undertaking any major scheme, the oracle would be consulted.

Mount Olympus is the home of the gods; it is the highest mountain in Greece and has 52 peaks and deep gorges. That sounds like plenty of room for the gods to think up their mischief.

The highest point is 9,570 feet, one of the highest peaks in Europe. People go there to admire the rich diversity of plant and animal life. Many birds use Greece as a stopping point on their annual migrations.

The scenery is stunning, and you can find Christian monasteries in awe-inspiring locations, including the highest orthodox chapel.

Greece has many museums with priceless artifacts from the ancient world as well as a vibrant modern artistic culture. Studying the myths of ancient Greece or other ancient civilizations and relating them to history is a very satisfying way to spend many hours.

BIRD WATCHING

Greece is placed at the crossroads of Asia, Europe, and Africa, so it provides shelter and rest for many species of migratory birds and has its own varied bird population. The Greek Ornithological Society works hard to protect endangered species, making it possible for birds and people to live in harmony. Holiday birding tours are popular, taking in some of the most beautiful scenery in the world.

Four hundred and forty-nine bird species have been spotted in Greece, and there are 196 areas designated as special for birds; these include wetlands, lagoons, and lakes. Wind farms have been prohibited in certain areas to protect the birds.

The best times for seeing the birds in Greece are when they migrate, which occurs in late April to early May in the spring, and the first half of September in autumn. And if you want to see the lesser white-fronted goose, go in November!

You may be lucky enough to see some spectacular birds, such as hundreds of Dalmatian and great white pelicans and greater flamingos – an awe-inspiring sight. To help vultures, the Hellenes provide vulture feeding stations; you may catch sight of Egyptian and griffon vultures.

Greece has a rich local bird population that includes species such as the masked shrike, Riuppell's warbler, and the spur-winged lapwing. Over 100,000 waterfowl winter on the Evros Delta, and there are many other bird-watching delights in Greece.

The good news is that bird watching can be done anywhere by anyone. Very often, there are local bird watch groups you can take part in. Gone are the days of people stealing eggs from wild birds' nests (Oology was considered a hobby where collectors collected bird eggs, but this is now illegal in most places); in the present day, it's all about conservation and ensuring our grandchildren can wake up to the dawn chorus.

Bird watching may encourage people to get up early and enjoy nature at its best before everyone else comes along. Groups can provide social friendships, lectures, and books that can increase your knowledge. Some apps translate the bird's song for you, so you know which elusive bird is singing its heart out to you.

And if you slow down the bird's song, very often, you will find a complete concerto there in all its amazing structure.

SUMMARY

In Greece, you are never far from the water, so swimming in the sea comes naturally. If you can make it one of your hobbies, it will both reward and refresh you.

Tavli are popular board games played on the sidewalks, and you could bring out your own board games and play with your neighbors on the street or in a park.

Greece is also famous for its ancient ruins and its mythology. Studying the gods and their many foibles would be a fascinating hobby, while studying archeology, with site visits where possible, could lead to many interesting conversations with fellow enthusiasts.

We don't typically pay much attention to olives. Yet, they have their own characteristics, and you could soon be an olive expert.

In many, many countries, bird watching is popular. Greece is at a bird migration crossroads, and there are many spectacular birds, some rarely seen. But bird watching is a hobby you can do in your own backyard and get hours of enjoyment, or the birds may lead you to explore new places and meet other birders.

> Swimming in the sea
> Tavli
> Olive appreciation
> Mythology
> Ancient history
> Bird watching

NEW ZEALAND

You will meet many active octogenarians in New Zealand. There seems to be no limit to the number of hobbies they have.

One unique characteristic of New Zealand culture is the contribution of the Māori culture. The Māori are the Indigenous Polynesian people of mainland New Zealand (Aotearoa), who originated with settlers from East Polynesia and arrived in New Zealand in several waves of waka (canoe) voyages between roughly 1320 and 1350.

Another unique characteristic is the country's pride in being self-contained, with its people trying to avoid contaminants and invasive species from the outer world, preserving their unique environment and way of life.

New Zealand is a beautiful country with stunning scenery and a pleasant climate, making it an attractive source of inspiration for many hobbies. Let's look at some of them now.

ECO GARDENING

Gardening is BIG in New Zealand. The temperate climate, the fertile soils, and the energy of the inhabitants make gardening one of the favorite pastimes for people of all ages. As a result, almost half the population indulges in gardening.

New Zealand has a vast range of bird and insect life, and many of its indigenous plants are also unique. However, since Europeans settled in New Zealand, they brought with them many plants, and some of them, like old man's beard and morning glory, became invasive.

Now there are extremely severe penalties for anyone attempting to bring seeds or plants into the country.

Ayrlies Garden

Ayrlies Garden is quintessential New Zealand. Starting in 1964, the countryside was then a bare paddock with heavy clay soil. Now, this six-star garden is one of the delights of New Zealand. It covers 12 acres and has informally planted borders plus lawns and waterways. There is also a wetland area for aquatic life and birds.

But let's give it a little twist and save the world! An ecologically designed garden uses local plants, minimizes waste, and avoids unnatural pesticides and chemicals. It needs intelligent and possibly innovative ideas to make the garden productive and environmentally friendly. Many gardens in New Zealand keep these principles in mind.

Stop digging!

Digging disturbs the microorganisms that live in the soil. So why do we need to dig? For countless eons, worms have been doing a very effective job – we should just let them get on with it. Mulching instead is much easier on your back.

Plant a tree

> *Warm are the winds in the woodlands*
> *Wafting their way through the leaves.*
> *Weaving and winding and whispering*
> *Like wind flowing over the sheaves.*
> *– Anglo Saxon poem*

If you have room, plant a tree. Trees are decorative and provide shade and perches for birds. Beneath a tree is a wonderful place to lie and gaze up at the sky through the pattern of leaves and branches.

Research the best plants and where to put them. Some like the sun, others shade, some like clay soil, others like sandy soil, some like floods, and others prefer to stay dry. It's fun learning about your locality and how to make your garden fruitful.

Recycle

If you can use recycled goods to make your fences and pathways, go for it. Also, unusual containers for potted plants can be decorative and add a talking point to your hobby.

Grow your own food

New Zealanders excel at this. Nothing is more satisfying than tasting that first home-grown raspberry or potato. You may have been eyeing that tomato for weeks: too small, still green... ready at last! And any excess can be preserved for the cold winter months.

Leave room for the original inhabitants

Man has been busy pushing out every conceivable type of wildlife and stealing their land, their sources of food, and their shelter. We owe it to them to make provision for them in our eco-gardens. And watching the antics of a squirrel or hearing the song of the birds can provide hours of entertainment.

Let a little part of your garden go back to nature – you will be surprised at the variety of pretty plants that take over, where dead wood provides homes for many insects, and what wildlife begins to move back in.

And it's all labor-free!

BEEKEEPING

Do you need a little helping hand with your garden? Why not try beekeeping?

One of New Zealand's most famous men was a commercial beekeeper – Edmund Hillary – the first man to stand on the top of Mount Everest in 1953 with Tenzing Norgay.

In 2019, there were 9217 registered beekeepers in New Zealand with over 800,000 hives. While many of these were commercial enterprises, this figure still suggests that beekeeping is a popular pastime.

Beekeepers in New Zealand subscribe to a voluntary code of conduct, which aims to ensure the sustainability of bees. This is important since bee populations have suffered, and the numbers have declined worldwide because of the use of toxic insecticides.

New Zealand is home to 28 species of native bees, and of these, 27 only occur in New Zealand. The other one also lives in Australia and somehow posted itself across to New Zealand, unaided by humans. These native bees are tiny – only 4 - 12 mm long – so they are easy to miss. They are also solitary creatures, nesting in the ground, but there are a lot of them.

Better known are the imported honeybees and bumblebees, which are bigger and better for commercial pollination. Altogether that makes 41 species of bees you can find in New Zealand. And it's these imported bees that beekeepers look after.

Before embarking on beekeeping, you need to understand what you are getting yourself into: there is a steep learning curve. You will need to enroll in beekeeping courses, not only to learn about bees but also to help establish your bee colony, and to provide you with the support of like-minded people afterward.

The bees will pollinate your garden and make your crops flourish, but we need to take care of them and protect them from the harsh chemicals that so many of us spray on our plants.

CANNING

When your garden is full of fantastic fruit and vegetables, it would be terrible not to use them. So, preserving by canning or bottling is popular in New Zealand.

Open kettle canning

This canning method is still prevalent in New Zealand. It involves putting hot food into a jar or can and then sealing it in without further treatment.

There is no current legislation in New Zealand covering home canning. However, there are stricter rules in America, where this type of kettle canning is considered unsafe, and all guidelines in America recommend processing after canning.

It is possible that *E. coli*, salmonella, and listeria can survive in unprocessed jars.

Methods of canning have evolved to make it safe, and if you decide to preserve your garden's produce, you will need to ensure you follow the recommended procedures and recipes.

You can buy proper supplies for canning and bottling, together with the lids. If you are considering buying supplies to preserve your produce, buying in multi-packs can save you money. Because the cost of jars is high in New Zealand, many people tend to reuse commercial containers.

Memories from an old-timer

"...we were able to sit down to peel them, then pack the peeled peaches into the jars while they were still raw. Then we poured a syrup of sugar and water over them, almost to the top of the jar. The perfect seal was placed on, and the screwband tightened just right. Then six jars were placed on a wire grid at the bottom of the preserver, with a seventh in the middle. Water was added to cover the jars by at least two inches, then the element was turned on, and the water was brought to the boil. After it boiled, a thermostat kept the water just at the boiling point for the required time. Twenty minutes for peaches..."

You can find plenty of information if you are interested in preserving your garden produce. It's ecologically satisfying and can give you and your family delicious home-grown fruit and vegetables.

BOARD GAMES

Board games are popular in New Zealand, and often people combine a board game with a night in with friends. Here are a few of the popular games:

Scrabble

Scrabble is prominent in New Zealand. It is great for spelling and vocabulary and is a very mentally stimulating game.

Pictionary

Pictionary is for all ages – and anyone with a sense of humor! It doesn't matter if you are not "artistic."

Monopoly

Monopoly started out as a teaching tool to show the dangers of concentrated land ownership, but makes for an exciting challenge with friends and family.

The Game of Life board game

In this game, the player can make choices as they move through life's challenges, so it is an excellent game for older people.

Cluedo

Do you like to solve a murder mystery? A game of logic, Cluedo is all about finding clues to find out "whodunnit."

There are many other games, but the New Zealand tradition is to invite other people into your home to play. It's better than being glued to the television.

BOOK CLUBS

In New Zealand, almost everyone belongs to at least one book club. Usually, people get together to discuss a book they have all been reading.

It does mean you have to get a copy of the book and maybe read something you would not have chosen yourself, but you can often get a brilliant surprise. Together with the visit, the coffee, and the biscuits, this can be an enjoyable and educational way to spend a few hours.

Often the book club extends into such things as garden visits, exploring different varieties of trees, and tasting unusual apples or pears. Recipes and tips for around the home, and lovely personal touches are special too. Or it can be formal and strictly about the book, maybe with someone reading part of the book, or perhaps a poem. You can sit back and enjoy the sound of their voice without distractions.

Some of the clubs have a theme – maybe, for example, animals or train engines – which can lead to exciting outings for members. Book clubs are as versatile as their members.

There is also an extensive range of virtual book clubs, so you can make friends with people from faraway places with a common interest. In addition, people living in a foreign country may find a book club is a great way to establish friendships with like-minded people, and improve their foreign language acquisition.

U3A

To continue with slightly academic subjects, many New Zealanders are members of U3A – the University of the Third Age. This will keep those grey cells active.

This started in Toulouse, France, and has spread all over the world. Some of the groups might be loosely attached to the local university, but more often, they are started by people who want to know more about life. And who better to tell them than the older people who have lived it.

Usually, people meet every month or so, and one of the local members or maybe a visiting expert will give a talk about a subject that interests them. It could be about their career, but it could equally be about their hobby.

The range of interesting subjects is infinite, and because the speakers themselves are enthusiasts, the way they impart their knowledge is often exciting as well as informative.

Often there will be a break for tea or coffee and a chat. You can meet some fascinating people here, folk who are intelligent and experienced in life. And you do not have to give your own little lecture unless you want to.

True words from Peter Laslett of U3A Cambridge, 1981, founder of the UK branch:

> *"Those who teach shall also learn.*
> *Those who learn shall also teach."*

U3As provide lifelong learning and sharing for retired and semi-retired people. Taking part might encourage you to step a little out of your comfort zone to take part in active learning and contribute.

Sometimes, mini-groups branch off, where people with particular interests can share their thoughts and knowledge. Examples might be art, archaeology, modern history, travel, and many more. These groups require an administrative backup – a committee, including a secretary, treasurer, newsletter writer, and organizer.

U3As may be run quite differently. For example, in France, the meetings tend to be led by working academics. However, in Britain, a more egalitarian approach was favored, focusing on self-help, which is usually the model followed in New Zealand.

CHOIRS

People in New Zealand love to sing together. Most New Zealanders have sung in school choirs, and more and more people are joining choirs as adults, rediscovering the joys of singing together. In fact, it is not unknown for people to join three choirs at once.

But there is more than just the joy of participation: there is the opportunity to excel for those who want it. National choirs like the New Zealand Youth Choir and the Voices New Zealand Chamber Choir have won international awards. Many ensembles travel overseas to sing. Soloists may also become world-renowned.

The New Zealand Choral Federation organizes an annual festival and competition for the choirs of secondary schools called The Big Sing. It lasts three days – and involves a tremendous amount of preparation and many, many rehearsals.

The pleasure of joining in, of taking part, producing some brilliant sounds, and perhaps even the possibility of winning competitions, makes joining a choir something the people of New Zealand love. Might there be a local choir in your neighborhood to sing with?

CROCHET CLUBS

Finally, for a more peaceful occupation, there are crochet and knitting clubs. There are many groups scattered all over New Zealand. It's not just a chance for a good natter: it's also about the sharing of skills and the final production of that gorgeous sweater or that cute little toy.

But it wasn't always quite so peaceful. Take the case of Henry Coutts. Queen Victoria herself crocheted four woolen scarves, which were awarded to four colonial soldiers for gallantry. While working in South Africa, Coutts risked his own life to rescue a mortally wounded non-commissioned officer from the Burmese Mounted Infantry. For this deed of valor, he received a gold star and clasp, plus one of the Queen's own crocheted scarves.

And don't think crochet is just an old lady's hobby. Take the case of Lissy Cole and Rudi Robinson-Cole's life-size crocheted wharenui (communal house of the Māori people of New Zealand.) This was inspired by Maori design, and the idea is to help people understand mātauranga Māori or Māori knowledge. This is an ongoing project and is expected to take over two years to complete. They hope to involve many Māori people in the work as well as international and local artists. This will spread joy in our lives, derived from Māori culture and insights.

Many charities, especially animal charities, are crying out for little crocheted or knitted toys to either sell or let the animals use as toys. Likewise, children's charities often desperately need gifts with a personal touch for children in need. Some charities want knitted blankets; there is a wide range of charitable concerns for people with the skills to help.

Crochet and knitting clubs are versatile, friendly places for people to share a pleasant few hours in the company of like-minded, artistic people, and no two clubs are exactly the same.

SUMMARY

New Zealand is full of people actively enjoying their many hobbies.

Eco-gardening not only cares for the planet but can also provide you with healthy food. And keeping bees to pollinate your crops makes good ecological sense, although there is a steep learning curve for new beekeepers.

And once you have grown your food, why not preserve it? Canning and bottling are both popular methods in New Zealand, and there are plenty of instructions on the internet to help you get started.

Then we have three activities to keep your brain supple. First, consider board games – there is a huge variety – something to suit almost anyone. There is U3A – the University of the Third age – if there is a group near you, join it for interesting talks and conversations. New Zealanders also enjoy book clubs – are there any near you? If not, why not create one?

Choirs not only let you sing, but also connect you with your fellow singers. The joint effort creates a great sound as well as gives a person a sense of belonging. And if all this is too much, how about joining a crochet group and producing some unique articles as well as having a good chin wag?

    Eco-gardening
    Beekeeping
    Canning and preserving
    Board games
    Book clubs
    U3A
    Choirs
    Crochet clubs

GERMANY

Television, radio, and surfing the internet have become increasingly popular ways for Germans to spend their leisure time. They are also great travelers, and if you meet a hardy tourist in an out-of-the-way place and wearing top-notch gear, the chances are he or she will be German.

Germany is a land rich in legend, with the secretive Black Forest and the beautiful Bavarian Alps. So, let us explore the things the German people like to do now.

TATORT

The Germans have organized a slightly different slant to watching television. Since 1970, a program called "Tatort" has been running continuously. Tatort means crime scene.

Around ten million Germans tune in every Sunday evening because it's more fun to watch it with company. Pubs have often organized public viewing sessions, and many participate by tweeting, in addition to watching and discussing.

It's a clever concept since different regional broadcasters take turns to produce the episodes, so the action takes place in different cities. That's one way to get to know your country.

RIVER CRUISES

Another way to know your country is to take a river cruise. And floating along the blue Danube or the river Rhine has all the delights you could wish for.

So, let's look at river cruises. These are smaller and more intimate than grand ocean liners, but they often provide a high level of comfort. Being closer to the scenery, you can get a good idea of the country you are passing through.

The beautiful blue Danube

You could travel along the Danube, which starts in Germany's Black Forest and, 1,785 miles further on, ends up in the Black Sea in Romania. It passes through four capital cities (Vienna, Bratislava, Budapest, and Belgrade) and is surrounded by the home cities of great composers like Mozart, Brahms, Beethoven – and of course, the Strauss family. You likely know "The Beautiful Blue Danube," the immortal waltz by Johann Strauss.

River Rhine cruises

Germany also offers river Rhine cruises. The river winds its way between fairy-tale castles perched on impossible cliffs and visits medieval towns on its way. The Rhine Gorge, the river's central section, has achieved World Heritage Site status.

There are mysterious legends as well as stunning scenery and historical interest to entice you. For example, Siegfried, the great German hero, allegedly slew a dragon on the shores of the river Rhine, and Lorelie, the water nymph, lives beneath the surface. And for decades, the river was the boundary between the Roman Empire and the barbarian hordes outside.

Some of the places you might visit include Strasbourg, with the soaring cathedral and the quaint canals; Cologne, for gothic spires as modern skyscrapers, as well as Koblenz with its dominating fortress.

Christmas cruises

Christmas cruises are special. You can sip your warm glühwein (mulled wine) with the scent of cinnamon as you watch the towns lit up for Christmas along the bank of the river. Then, stop off at a Christmas market, where you can buy all you want for a festive celebration. Snow sets off sparking lights, and as darkness falls, the air seems magical. You will likely hear carols or maybe sleigh bells as Father Christmas visits.

GEOCACHING

Geocaching is a fairly new outdoor activity that has taken off globally. It's a treasure hunt with a modern twist.

Geocachers give clues for those seeking the "treasure," or geocache, a small, waterproof treasure box hidden somewhere outdoors. The modern twist is that every geocache also has global positioning system (GPS) coordinates, which get the treasure hunters to within 50 feet.

Today over 1.4 million geocaches have been hidden, and over 4 million people worldwide have taken part in hunting them down. And Germany, together with America, is a world leader.

This can be an exciting outdoor activity, and anyone can take part; you might go solo, do it as a family outing or join a small group. You might compete with others; there are many possibilities. And you learn about new places as well.

You need a GPS and a waterproof bag to collect any rubbish. There are strict ecological rules:

- The geocache must not be buried anywhere where it might cause damage or harm.
- The geocache must be safe – no knives or explosives, drugs or food.
- Local regulations must be respected, and local signs obeyed.
- The local environment must not be altered.
- People should not need to cut back vegetation or disturb nesting sites to find the treasure.

The most popular geocache in the world is in Prague, in the Czech Republic, but Germany has a fantastic site in Baden-Württemberg, which offers a five-stage multi-cache – quite a challenge.

Entry is often free, but it does take time and expense to set up a cache.

TOY VOYAGERS

The inspiration for the toy voyagers was from the film *Amélie*, which featured a traveling gnome. Could toys go places, see the world and meet people?

This has become a global community for toys and their hosts in various countries, including Germany. There are over 6000 members, and more than 3000 toys have been sent on their travels to 148 countries.

Hosts offer places for the toys to stay, but toy hosts do more than that: they give their little guests a guided tour of places of local interest, take photos and post them on the toy's own travelogue.

You can put in requests for toy hosts to send your little toy too, and your toy may then be returned or sent on further adventures.

To give your toy the opportunity of a lifetime, register him or her with ToyVoyagers.com. You can also browse the travel logs of other toys, and it can be fascinating to follow the adventures of these little travelers.

Once registered, your toy will have its own travel log, which its hosts can update. And if it has its own bucket list, maybe there will be a host out there happy to help.

It's an excellent way for you to travel the world without any of the discomforts, delays, and documentation associated with travel.

GARDEN GNOMES

"Gartenzwerg" is German for "garden dwarf," but the biggest gnome is nearly 18 feet tall! Most garden gnomes are a more manageable size of between one and two feet tall.

There are about 25 million garden gnomes in Germany. Originally they were manufactured in Germany, but the gnomes are now often imported from China or Poland, and there is a huge variety in type and price. And if you think they can be slightly brash, know that they were originally made to decorate the gardens of wealthy people in Europe and are now popular with all social classes.

Their history is a surprisingly ancient one. In Rome, an idol of the god of fertility was often placed in gardens. During the renaissance period, Paracelsus described gnomes as "diminutive figures two spans in height who did not like to mix with humans." Garish stone statues, including the Gobbo, or hunchbacks, adorned (if that is the right word) the gardens of the rich.

Then, in the 1700s, these little folk became entwined with the legends of Germany, and many were thought to bring good luck to farms and mines. In Dresden, the first ceramic dwarves were created in 1841 – possibly the first actual garden gnomes?

Their popularity rapidly spread, and one early gnome, called "Lampy," produced in England, is now on show at Lamport Hall and is insured for £1 million! Yet, for a time, gnomes were banned from the prestigious Chelsea Flower Show in England.

Snow White and the Seven Dwarves created a surge in interest and lower prices. And the gnomes might travel as well: there was a "hobby" of stealing a gnome, taking a photo, and then returning the gnome plus a photo to the owner. Another kind of toy voyager!

You can find every kind of garden gnome, although traditionally, they are bearded males. Many are funny, slightly grotesque, or even evil-looking. Take your pick, but collecting garden gnomes can be strangely satisfying and it can make for an entertaining walk with your grandchildren to go see the gnomes.

SUMMARY

Germany is a land of legend but also very modern. The hobbies reflect this dual personality.

Taking inspiration from Tatort, communal watching of television shows turns a solitary occupation into a fun social gathering.

Another modern twist is the geocaching treasure hunt. This can take you to places you might not otherwise even know existed.

But going back in time, river cruises take in some remarkable scenery and extraordinary castles, each with its own legends. And if you don't fancy a river cruise, you can bring some of the mythology into your own backyard by installing a dwarf or three.

Toy voyaging is yet another way to explore the world by sending off your toy to do the hard traveling – they will be well looked after by other toy voyaging experts.

> Tatort
> River cruises
> Geocaching
> Toy voyagers
> Garden gnomes

AUSTRIA

Austria has a rich and varied history together with beautiful mountains in the south and rich plains in the north. Cycling, family walks, and eating out are some of the ways Austrians spend their free time.

Arts and crafts are popular, and Austrians produce lovely homemade jewelry. Singing, dancing, and music echoes off the hills. They yodel in the mountains; in their leather shorts, they dance the Schuhplattler with energetic knee-slapping. They engage in folk music with accordions and a double-necked guitar, and of course, there is the legacy of the immortal Mozart and the renowned Haydn.

Vienna is known as the City of Music: composers lived there, stayed there, and wrote awe-inspiring music in Vienna. There are many venues for concerts and theatre, and Vienna is also famed for electronic music.

Here are just five of the many hobbies available.

THEATRE

Vienne and Salzburg are sophisticated cities with many concert halls, opera houses, and theatres. Each has its annual festivals, lasting several weeks.

The first Salzburg Festival Hall was set up in 1925 in an archbishop's stables. Salzburg was the birthplace of Wolfgang Amadeus Mozart, and both music and drama were featured there. One of the highlights is the annual performance of the play "Jedermann" (Everyman) by Hugo von Hofmannsthal.

Vienna has the Burgtheater (the Imperial Court Theatre), the national theatre of Austria, one of the most important theatres in the German language and has a checkered history. It was originally built in an old tennis court in 1540 and was reopened in 1741 by the empress who wanted a theatre next to her palace. It was then relocated again in 1888, destroyed by American bombing in 1945, and rebuilt once more in 1955. The Burgtheater has developed its unique style and is considered to be at the forefront of German theatre.

But newer musical traditions have also arisen in Austria. In 1967, the first international annual hip hop festival was started in Salzburg. This festival features new works and attracts local and international hip-hop artists.

But what could be nicer than a group of friends visiting the local theatre? You have an opportunity to dress up, a chance to gossip and catch up on the local scandal, and even to improve your mind.

There are so many local theatre groups putting on shows and wanting audiences. Sometimes the outing can involve overnight stays and a chance to make new friends and store up a good memory to look back on.

YODELING

Yodeling is fun but not something to be practiced in your living room unless you live a considerable distance from anyone else!

In Napoleonic times, yodeling in the Tyrol Alps in Austria was used as a gesture of defiance to the French troops. Meanwhile, yodeling became assimilated into folk music in neighboring Switzerland, and festivals were organized to celebrate local traditions.

In both countries, yodeling was seen as patriotic, especially in Nazi Austria. Switzerland was eager to produce its own brand of yodeling to differentiate it from any others and distance itself from the Nazi ideology.

In the 1960s and 1970s, yodeling was seen as somewhat ridiculous, but a revival has taken place, and yodeling is now a popular pastime. It is undoubtedly a great way to relieve stress and communicate with other people at international workshops.

And yodeling carries a long way – one can imagine a leather-shorted mountaineer yodeling across the valleys to a friend on the opposite side.

I'm not too sure what a spouse or partner will think of you taking up yodeling, but I will leave it to your own discretion. It sounds fun to me!

ACCORDION PLAYING

When you visit Austria, you will meet an accordion player, whether you like it or not. Invented in Austria, this versatile instrument is the backbone of traditional folk music, especially in mountainous regions.

The traditional Austrian Schrammelmusik ensemble is made up of accordion, guitar, clarinet, and fiddle. You hear them in country fairs; you will see them on local parades; and in the evenings you can watch them on stage accompanying folk dancing. Orchestras in Vienna developed their own kind of blues, "the Viennese Blues," in which the accordion played enthusiastically.

Naturally, there are accordion festivals, including one in Vienna where 200 accordionists meet and play for a month of varied music on various accordions – the squeezebox, the concertina, or even the hand-organ.

The accordion is loud. It is also versatile and has a happy sound – it makes you want to smile, get up, and dance. I have vivid memories of myself with my friend Cindy, learning to play the accordion from her family members while visiting Europe. We had such fun; we were full of smiles!

JEWELRY MAKING FROM SCRAP (OR KITS)

Austria is home to some beautiful hand-made jewelry, but it's not all made from scrap.

Schullin's studio is just one of the places in Austria where you can find modern designs made using traditional crafting methods. This family business has been operating since 1802.

They start with the rough stone and customize the finished item to the buyer's personal taste. They even use digital 3D modeling to ensure the piece is perfect.

But nearly anyone can learn to make jewelry, and you don't need to buy expensive supplies. Instead, you can buy kits with readymade beads, gems, silver wear, and all the tools you need to make breath-taking jewelry pieces.

More challenging and possibly even more engrossing is making jewelry from scrap. It's amazing what you can do with a safety pin and a sample of material or homemade paper beads.

It's still best to make sure you have the tools you need to cut wire and thread strings.

Your hobby provides you with unique and thoughtful gifts or items you will be proud to wear yourself. You might even be able to sell them, although that is a tough market to enter.

The concentration needed and the focus required are wonderful ways to alleviate stress, and it doesn't take up much room in your home.

SUMMARY

This cheerful little country is also the venue for music, theatre, and artisans producing beautiful jewelry.

You can make your own jewelry from scraps, and the only limit is your own imagination.

Learning to play the accordion could be interesting – it's loud and cheerful, and why not yodel? Who can make the best sounds in your family? (But in both cases, be wary of annoying your neighbors since these sounds are meant to travel.)

For something a little different, you could always emulate the Schuhplattler dance.

But for a classy evening out, the theatre can be an elegant and social occasion.

>Theatre groups
>Yodelling
>Accordion playing
>Jewelry from scrap or kits

SINGAPORE

M odern Singapore was founded in 1964, but its past extends to the 7th century when Buddhist-Hindu empires made their homes there. It is a tiny island off the southern tip of Malaya, which you can drive all the way across in half an hour. Its name means "lion city" in Sanskrit, although there were never lions in Singapore.

Although the official language is Malay Bahasa, the government uses English for official communications. However, many of the locals speak "Singlish," a local combination of languages derived from English with additions from Chinese and Teochew.

Singapore has some amazing sites crammed into such a small space, including the famous Gardens by the Bay, the inspiration for the film Avatar. Lit up in red, blue, and purple lights, it attracts thousands of visitors.

Despite its relatively short history, Singapore, with its six million inhabitants, has grown rapidly from a poor agricultural country without industry or natural resources to being placed in the top ten wealthiest countries globally. Business is incredibly efficient, and the people of Singapore have turned this strategic shipping point into a worldwide technological innovation hub.

So what do the island people do in their spare time?

JOURNALING AND BLOGGING

Life is fast-paced and can be stressful for many people. Journaling is an excellent way to relieve stress and also keep a record of your life. And if you feel comfortable sharing your thoughts, blogging is also a great option to keep connected with the world around you.

There are many different forms of the journal, and in Singapore, you can find them all. A favorite seems to be the bullet journal or "BuJo." This usually has sections for your to-do list, calendars, recording your health and exercise, plus a written section for your goals. Keeping track of how you feel and your actions are conducive to good time management – a feature of the efficient people of Singapore.

Singaporeans have paid workshops to help people make the best BuJo they can. They explore the concept of journaling, its presentation, tools you might find helpful, and what to do when you make a mistake.

But there are many other types of journals. You can share them, communicate through them or just relax on the couch with them. Some examples might include:

- Project journal
- Travel journal
- Diet journal
- Dream journal

And there are many more.

Keeping a journal can help you "see the forest for the trees." It's so easy to forget what is important to you, and a journal can remind you why you get up in the morning.

One tip is to buy a nice book to write your thoughts in – it makes it special.

Blogging comes naturally when you live on a small, crowded, yet prosperous island. Singapore has a multitude of blogging websites, and some of them are very well known. Blogging can be a great way to express yourself as a hobby, and you can add in social media to market your blog if you wish to do so.

Digitalization has transformed the way we communicate worldwide, and Singapore has taken full advantage of this. Of course, you need skill and perseverance to create a successful blog, but what a wonderful way to meet all kinds of people from all over the world online. You can share your recipes – like the hot chili crab of Singaporean fame – you can moan about just about anything and debate with people thousands of miles away or just next door.

Common topics include health and beauty, films and media, and travel. In fact, there is something for everyone from this tiny land.

VIRTUAL REALITY

Singapore is one of the most technologically advanced and connected countries globally and is at the forefront of new and exciting digital technologies.

While nothing can beat the real thing, a virtual reality, or VR experience can get you pretty close nowadays. Internet and virtual reality cafes are popping up all over Singapore, opening up opportunities and experiences to individuals of all ages.

A computer isn't necessary; you may need to invest in some electronic hardware, but even some newer smartphones can do the trick on their own. Your local community might even have some VR cafes so you can try things out before making an investment, and not have to bother with the technical end of things yourself. VR headsets slide over your eyes and block everything else out, so make sure you have a comfortable and safe area available!

Before you know it, you will be attending virtual concerts, touring famous museums, and seeing priceless exhibits in locations far from home. And it doesn't have to just be by yourself: these virtual experiences can also be enjoyed with family, neighbors, or friends from around the world.

Make it a group event to attend virtual workout classes, enjoy relaxing meditation experiences, or visit favorite childhood landmarks. Having a virtual meet-up with family overseas can feel like you are all in the same room together again.

Or, if mobility is holding you back, you could relive experiences from your youth that your body is no longer up for, like playing a demanding sport or going on a safari. And if you're feeling more adventurous, you could try things you would never have imagined doing in real life, like scaling the highest mountaintops, skydiving, or bungee jumping, all without the danger.

COLLECTING PLASTIC BAGS

This might not sound like a fun hobby, but plastic kills marine animals and birds and damages our oceans and environment. With Singapore's small size, they are conscious of their limited landfill space, and thus recycling is encouraged.

Despite some limitations in their recycling program, there are places in Singapore that accept plastic bags and other junk for craftwork. This is where collecting plastic bags can become an interesting hobby.

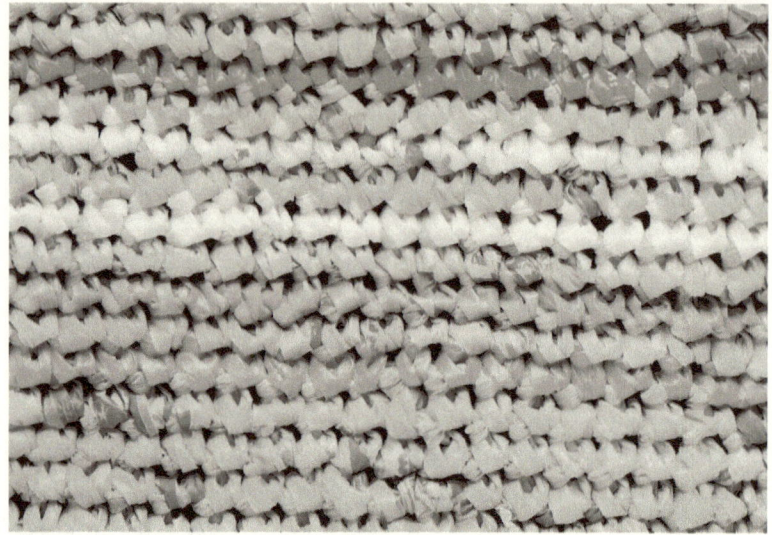

The bags come in so many colors and can be made into so many items for further use. Decorative mats and woven baskets are just two; you can probably think of many more. And as you collect the bags and recycle them, you are also doing your bit for the environment.

I am not thinking of the beach cleanups many volunteers in maritime countries engage in – incredibly useful and wonderful social occasions though they are – rather, this is collecting new or nearly new bags that would otherwise be dumped in landfill sites, polluting our planet.

SUMMARY

Singapore has a vibrant and energetic community, with some common hobbies. Common hobbies in Singapore reflect the industrious nature of its inhabitants. You might try journaling to keep your brain active and organized, blogging, perhaps to make money, but more usually to share your own experiences and knowledge and open lines of communication worldwide. Collected plastic bags can be made into various attractive and useful items, or you could choose something else to recycle into a homemade creation.

    Journaling and blogging
    Virtual reality
    Collecting plastic bags

ITALY

I taly is so rich in culture that we are spoilt for choice. Everywhere there is stunning scenery from the vertical cliffs of the red-rocked Dolomites in the north to the sandy beaches and blue seas of the south, and the pastures and villages, churches, and vineyards up and down the countryside. Italy is a Catholic country, so many of the works of art are religious, and many of the finest murals and sculptures are to be found in the churches.

Italy has an enormous archaeological heritage, from the Greeks and the Romans, with some of the world's most famous art being produced in the medieval and renaissance periods. Italy has been home to incomparable artists like Michelangelo and Botticelli, along with scientists like Galileo and Da Vinci making contributions to mankind.

We are fortunate that so much of Italy's history has survived to enchant us today. Here is a small selection of hobbies and interests that are popular in Italy that you might like to try.

CHESS

You may not associate chess with Italy, but they have a different slant on it – living chess.

In the pretty hill town of Marostica, people can watch a re-enactment of a live chess duel. It all started back in 1454. Lord Tadio Parisio had a beautiful daughter named Leonora. Two noblemen both wanted her hand in marriage, so the lord organized a live chess game – the winner could take Leonora, but the loser had to take the hand of his younger daughter Oldrada (killing two birds with one stone). He held a grand parade with flags and fireworks and a great feast.

History does not record how the two young ladies felt. But ever since then, every two years, the live chess game is re-enacted on the pink and white marble slabs embedded in the center of the piazza, which form a chessboard. This event has parades, banners, and exotic costumes, as well as the game itself, and tickets to watch are a sellout.

Chess has been around for nearly 1500 years. The game probably originated in India; from there, it spread to Persia. Then, it carried on in the Muslim world and reached southern Europe with the Moorish conquest of Spain. Now it is one of the most popular and intellectually demanding games in the world.

This really is a case of use it or lose it. Playing mentally demanding games such as chess has been shown to keep our brains in working order, so it's an excellent hobby for older people with the time and patience to work out strategies and tactics and the competitive nature to outwit your opponent.

If you can't find a chess club or local competition, you can also play against a computer. Even the computers play against each other in the World Computer Chess Championship. But as a hobby, chess can be stimulating and relaxing. What could be nicer than settling down with an old friend or with your grandchild for a friendly game of chess?

MOSAICS

Mosaics are an art form requiring the placement of small pieces of colored glass, minerals, shells, tiles, stones, or other materials closely together to form a pattern or picture. Walls and floors can be adorned in this way, and the multifaceted art can result in a shimmering and quite stunning image, which seems almost alive.

The oldest mosaic we know of dates from the third millennium BCE in Mesopotamia, but mosaics were popular in ancient and Byzantine Roman times.

When Mount Vesuvius erupted in 79 CE, the pyroclastic flow buried the small town of Herculaneum (as well as smothering Pompeii). Among the findings is the House of Neptune, a small, richly decorated townhouse. At the very back of the house, there was a courtyard with a garden, a grotto, and a fountain. On the back wall is a stunning mosaic, in vivid blues, featuring Neptune. One can imagine the family retiring to this peaceful haven after a long, hot day to relax and unwind.

But it's the town of Ravenna where the most awesome mosaics can be seen. Among the many churches with mosaics is the sixth-century Basilica of San Vitale. Here, the mosaic is a political statement depicting the emperor Justinian as central to the church's power and the military and imperial powers.

You can find mosaic floors even in the far-flung corners of the Roman Empire. But wherever they are located, the mosaics often have a deliberate fault, for to be perfect was to challenge the gods.

Nowadays, the peaceful focus required to place the mosaic pieces with care can be a fantastic way to create lasting beauty. Mosaics do not have to be floors or walls; they can decorate small surfaces, making, for example, a beautiful and unique box – maybe using the shells from a seaside visit to make a lasting memento.

Sometimes a community project might use a mosaic to decorate a railway station wall, as in Brighton, UK, where a workshop for children is producing a colorful mosaic. So this is a hobby to share or to work on solo.

Creating the lasting beauty of a scintillating, multifaceted mosaic can be enormously satisfying. And there are kits for sale and books of instructions just waiting for people to enjoy putting together mosaics as a hobby.

HAND GESTURES

Have you ever watched an Italian talk? It's fascinating. They seem to talk with their hands. And other Italians understand what the hands are saying.

Here are a few of the gestures an Italian may use, but be aware that they are open to misinterpretation and may mean different things in different parts of Italy. Nonetheless, it can be fun to try them out with friends and maybe make up your own system of signals.

So what?

Run your fingers up your neck and past the tip of your chin.

Idiot

Fingers point to your temple – we all know this one!

What do you mean?

Put your fingers together and point them upwards. Hold out your arm a foot away from your body and maybe move your hand up and down, or hold it still.

Finger kiss

Place your fingers together. Kiss them. This means "well done."

Please help

Make a prayer – put your hands together as if praying in front of your chest.

Perfect

Press your index finger to your thumb and draw a straight line in the air horizontally.

But remember, for the Italian, these gestures come naturally – and in other countries, the same gesture might mean something entirely different. You could make up your own, or incorporate some useful bits from your country's sign language. If you make a hobby of hand gestures, it might change the way you speak!

ART AND SCULPTURE APPRECIATION

It isn't easy to know where to start with art in Italy. Everywhere you go, you can find churches with treasures in them as well as museums with priceless works of art and sculptures.

Perhaps the greatest sculptor of all time was Michelangelo, and these are his words: "I saw the angel in the marble and carved until I set him free." He felt that every block of stone had a statue inside it, and it was the sculptor's task to find it.

One cannot fail to be moved by his "Pieta" or be impressed by his David. Yet, Michelangelo is perhaps even better known for his painting on the ceiling of the Sistine chapel.

There are other tremendously gifted Italians; Leonardo da Vinci comes to mind. He not only painted perhaps the most famous portrait of all time, the Mona Lisa, but he also created an airplane that could fly (he died in 1519). His painting of the Last Supper is almost equally famous and very beautiful, full of emotion and color. Much of his work was as an engineer for war machines, but he also worked as a scientist and architect.

While you may not be able to create works of art like the great Italian artists and sculptors of the past, you can appreciate them, and art appreciation is an amazingly insightful hobby. Once you begin to study paintings, you begin to understand a little of their history, and for those of you interested in how the paints were mixed, how the canvas was prepared, and so on, there is much fascinating detail to be found.

If you go to a sculpture museum, try blindfolding yourself and then feeling the exhibits, if this is permitted. You will get a totally different sensation and feel the piece at a deeper level of your consciousness.

We are fortunate that there are so many images we can look at in books and on the internet and physically visit museums and art galleries. This is a hobby with endless possibilities and is a way of communicating with people of long ago.

OPERA

Wherever you go in Italy, you will hear people singing. From open windows, from balconies, from the gondoliers, as they move along the canals in Venice, you will listen to a full-bodied song.

When you go to the opera in Italy, it is like nowhere else. The audience is part of the occasion. It's a time to wear your best clothes and be seen. Italy is famous for opera. Many famous composers were Italian, people like Puccini, Rossini, Paganini, and Monteverde, to name just four. The most performed opera in the world is La Traviata by Giuseppe Verdi, another Italian composer.

Now imagine it is a warm autumn evening, and the sky is dark. You enter the colosseum and maybe sit far back. There are 50,000 people in the audience. There is a buzz of anticipation, then silence, and far down below, the cast appears, and you can hear every word. This is because the acoustics are so good. Real horses and camels appear on stage; the opera Aida is in full flow. And when the opera ends, as it must, the audience comes to life, as only an Italian audience can.

But not to be outdone, the Italians have devised a modern type of opera, Opera buffa (comic opera), which is funny, modern, and may even include popular tunes. This contrasts to the "Opera seria" (tragic or dramatic opera), so there is something for everyone.

Singing is a well-known way to relax and open up your heart. The Italians do it in real style, but why can't you engage in opera? You could join a club or simply listen and maybe collect opera recordings.

Singing in your bath along with the rollicking tunes or declaring your hopeless love for a damsel can be very empowering!

SUMMARY

Italy is a land of song and art, from the gondoliers singing as they ply their gondolas in the canals of Venice to the fabulous sculptures and art in Rome and Florence, and everywhere you go.

Live chess is an interesting way to play this popular game, but an ordinary chessboard, a good partner, and a lot of patience will stimulate your grey cells, which might help keep your brain young.

Mosaics are an art form we tend to skip over, yet Italy has some brilliant examples, and it is something you can easily take up using natural materials close at hand or buying kits – there are plenty of them.

The art and sculpture of Italy are awe-inspiring. You may not be able to paint the ceiling of the Vatican (although one artist has painted a reproduction in a local church), but everyone can appreciate art. Visits to local art galleries and museums, plus the extraordinary variety of art books, make this a hobby that gives endless delight.

Hand gestures are natural to Italians, but they can be fun to try to make yourself understood, and if you learn sign language that the deaf can understand, that could be a bonus.

Finally, there is the opera. In Italy, opera houses are full, and the audience participates. Live opera is an experience not to be missed. Even at home, there may be a seemingly endless supply of vinyl, CDs, radio, and digital music you can enjoy; sing along as that usually makes us feel happy.

> Chess
> Mosaics
> Hand signals
> Art and sculpture appreciation
> Opera

DENMARK

Denmark is a small country, made up of a peninsula and many small islands with beautiful, sandy beaches. Danes are seafaring travelers by nature and have left their mark on many faraway places. Despite being small, Denmark claims the largest island in the world that is not a continent – Greenland – as part of the Kingdom of Denmark.

Denmark also has the longest combined rail and road bridge in Europe, five miles long, connecting the Danish capital, Copenhagen, with Sweden. And, of course, we cannot forget the little mermaid statue in Copenhagen.

So, let's look at some of the hobbies that Danish people enjoy or have enjoyed in the past.

RUNES

The Danes are a part of the Scandinavian group of Vikings, a seafaring people who traveled far and left their mark in the form of runes – Viking graffiti – which you can still find in some surprising places today.

No one knows where runes originated, but it is thought they are not older than 100 CE, possibly arising in Germanic tribes north of the Black Sea and spreading as the Goths and Huns came west. After that, runes were adopted by the Scandinavian peoples, including those living in Greenland and Iceland and the Sami of Lapland. It was the only writing we know of around 300 CE in Scandinavia, while the Latin script superseded it in the rest of Europe.

Runes could be read from right to left, from left to right, or even upside down, and as mirror images. Punctuation appears to be minimal. All runes are uppercase. But they could look very decorative when well written by a master. Maybe some of them were the magic formulae for spells and charms?

Like today, graffiti writing was a popular pastime, and the Norsemen left their mark far and wide. One of the best-known examples of their doodling is in Istanbul in the famous mosque of Hagia Sophia. Two bored Vikings left their names, Halfdan and Ari. It is not impossible that these two characters worked as bodyguards for the Byzantine Emperor. Vikings left their runes in Orkney and Scotland, and the biggest runes are found in Denmark and Sweden.

Discovering runes and trying to decipher them can be quite engaging, and there are books all about runes for anyone interested in Viking graffiti.

LEGO

Ole Kirk Christiansen worked as a carpenter in Billund, Denmark. He began making wooden toys around 1932 to supplement his income, and by 1934 his company took the name of Lego, which translates as "play well" in Danish. The original blocks were made from wood.

Soon after, Christiansen imported the technology to make injection-molded plastics. Lego has been plastic since 1949, but modern developments keep the company ahead as a world leader in producing toy building blocks.

In Denmark, you can spend two or three days visiting the workshops and getting an inside view of how Lego is produced, and you can see inside Christiansen's original house. You can meet the Lego workers and designers. There are exhibitions of Lego sets and original models, and you can even take part in building your own unique design.

In 1968, Legoland Billund resort opened – a theme park built entirely of Lego. And now there are theme parks in many parts of the world: Europe, North America, the Middle East, and Asia. You can visit the Arc de Triomphe in Paris; you look down on Big Ben and Buckingham Palace in London; there are many other famous places you can see – all in miniature, all made from Lego. You can also enjoy exciting attractions and water rides in a Lego theme park. It takes millions of bricks to build a Legoland park, and what an interesting job, designing and maintaining these exhibits.

But you don't have to go out of your home to enjoy Lego. You can get creative with a box of mini bricks, mini engines, and your own imagination or an instruction manual to guide you. Who knows what you will end up with? Lego isn't just absorbing for kids: it can be an entertaining hobby for anyone.

RANDOM ACTS OF KINDNESS

Random acts of kindness occur worldwide, but Denmark has a special place in this for two reasons: hygge and escape.

How do you define a random act of kindness? It's providing unprompted help, often to strangers, without expecting any reward except that it makes you feel good. Kindness helps us as individuals to reduce stress on both giver and receiver, as your brain releases the "feel-good" hormones. Acts of kindness also help build up a sense of community and change the world we live in for the better. Nowhere are they better demonstrated than the escape of the Jews in April 1940.

When the Nazis overran Denmark, the Danes, being independent thinkers, decided to save the Jews, and over 90% of

Danish Jews were deported, not to Nazi concentration camps, but to neutral Sweden, in small, crowded fishing boats. Within days, most of the Jews in Denmark had escaped. And it was ordinary Danes who cooperated in hundreds of small acts of kindness. This was an awe-inspiring feat.

The Danes continue to cooperate in kindness today, and farmers are required by law to put aside 5% of their land to grow field flowers for the bees.

Is it so surprising, then, that according to the World Happiness Report, Denmark is in the top three happiest countries to live in? The Danes have a concept, "hygge," built into their character and hard to translate. It roughly means finding comfort, pleasure and warmth in simple, soothing things. This concept spreads beyond the Danish shores, which is a surprise to many Danes since it is integral to their character. They use the word "hygge" in everyday speech without thinking about it.

With their excellent work-life balance, Danes have time and energy to do things they enjoy, whether that is knitting socks or running around the block. Hygge has a unique meaning to everyone.

But you don't have to be in Denmark to start a random act of kindness! These lovely acts are happening everywhere, and even a smile can be a gift to a lonely or sad person. Sometimes, the giver asks the receiver to pass on their own act of kindness to spread these good feelings.

Of all the hobbies in this book, this has to be the simplest and most rewarding.

FAIRY TALES

When you think of fairy tales, you probably think of Hans Christian Andersen. Born a poor cobbler's son, he died rich and famous. Spinning words to make multi-layered yarns, his tales have a charm and sophistication all of their own. With worldwide renown as simple fairy tales with all the aspects that children love, you may be forgiven for thinking his fairy tales lack depth, but look a little closer. You can find the hidden messages of philosophy and wisdom behind the simple translations.

The earliest fairy tales were of magic, ways of explaining and perhaps trying to placate the sometimes-hostile environment: a world where the shamans and bards had power and long, long memories. Often in praise of kings and rulers now forgotten, they encompassed all the elements of desire, fear, appeasement, and prowess of heroes and damsels. Myth and magic were inextricably intertwined with the tales of bravery and the long antecedents of rulers – now themselves lost in the mists of time.

Hans Anderson was a shrewd observer of people, and how they behaved. He was a serious craftsman: his tales are based on human nature with all its failings and heroism, set against the background of 19th century Denmark. He wrote 156 stories that have been translated into over 125 languages – you probably recognize some of them: Thumbelina, The Princess, and the Pea, and every boy's favorite, The Emperor's New Clothes. Anderson's bronze statue sits at the corner of "H. C. Andersens Boulevard," the most densely trafficked artery in central Copenhagen, Denmark.

Writing fairy tales for your own amusement or your grandchildren stimulates your imagination. For many children, going to bed involves the ritual of reading a story, and very often, they beg you to tell them your own story, and they listen with rapt attention. So why not write a few down and make your own book for them? Maybe they will pass your book of fairy tales onto their own children's children. You are famous at last!

SUMMARY

Demark is a seafaring nation, and they have left their mark in distant places, sometimes as graffiti in their runic writing. Runes can make an interesting study; you could even write your own.

The country is perhaps best known for the world-renowned Lego. Together with the add-on mini-engines, these little plastic bricks can make an engrossing pastime, and not just for children.

The grandkids will love the fairy tales you write. Hans Christian Anderson wrote many ever-popular stories, and now you could too.

But perhaps the very best hobby from all countries is the random acts of kindness, and in setting the example, Denmark is an inspiration to us all.

> Runes
> Lego
> Random acts of kindness
> Fairy tale writing

CHINA

China is a vast and beautiful country with a long and impressive history. Many of the world's inventions were first produced in China. What is most remarkable is how the mind and body are both involved in many of their hobbies.

The calm focus needed for calligraphy and Tai Chi, the relaxing effects of indoor waterfalls and Feng Shui, and its people's respect for their families – past and present – make China a country full of interest and delight.

We can only offer a snippet of their incredible range of interests and hobbies here.

FENG SHUI

Feng shui means "the way of wind and water." The very words are emotive. The art of feng shui originates in China, but is spreading worldwide, although, for a while, it was made illegal in China by the ruling communist party around 2005. Luckily it has made a comeback.

Feng shui has roots in early Taoism in the third and fourth centuries BCE.

What is the purpose of Feng Shui?

We can adjust our homes to instill a feeling of calmness to soothe our minds and nurture our bodies. It's a practical way of looking after our souls and being in harmony with our environment.

It is not a religion; it is not a belief system; it is not even superstition.

Feng shui may affect where we place our furniture, how we deal with clutter, and even the design of our window frames to make our homes better places to live in. But, if you get it wrong, it can adversely affect you, according to feng shui principles.

When you go shopping, you find that many large stores are set out in a very specific manner, scientifically tested to encourage you to spend money.

Here's an example in your home: if the bathroom door opens directly opposite the kitchen area, does it not feel a trifle unclean?

Similarly, if a coffee table has very sharp corners that you must carefully pass by every time you sit, does this feel uncomfortable or unsafe?

Keeping clutter well under control is also a part of feng shui. It feels good to lay your hands immediately on whatever it is you are looking for.

Some things you can do

You do not have to change your house or turn it sideways, but how you place your furniture, mirrors, and lighting can make a difference, and so can the colors you choose.

For example, it's said that if a doctor wants to shorten the number of people waiting, he will paint the reception area red in the hope that some patients will get too impatient and leave; if a therapist wants you to relax, the reception area will be a calm green or blue.

Windows are a key feature. It is nurturing to look outside at trees and the sky, but the right curtains or the right color frame can make a difference.

Do you need to cancel out noise with an extra glass layer? Or can you have your windows open any time of day?

Furniture placing

A sofa against a wall feels more secure when you are resting on it. It can be disturbing if people continually walk around the back of your sofa.

Can you see the doorway from your desk? When the door opens, we tend to see who is there, and it's easier if you do not have to turn your head.

There are many ways to enhance your home, guided by feng shui, an excellent little hobby to make you feel better.

INDOOR WATERFALLS

What is more peaceful than the sound of water flowing gently in an indoor fountain?

An indoor fountain can be a part of feng shui, and you can design and make them yourself. You might even make them for your friends – an unusual gift – or even sell them.

Waterfalls, fountains, and aquariums can give your office or home positive energy; make sure they are in the best place for them. They are said to attract good luck, and we all need a bit of that! Flowing water means life, enthusiasm, and helps you center yourself. And if you have air conditioning, this helps stop the air from drying out and becoming too arid.

But first, a couple of record breakers:

At Singapore's Changi Airport, in the new extension, there is the "rain vortex." This stunning waterfall is seven stories high and pumps 500,000 liters of rainwater down through the roof in a spectacular show.

But this record won't stand for long. The Eden Project is reaching out from England for its first international project in China's Shandong province. It will host the world's largest indoor waterfall, 50 meters high (nearly as high as the Niagara Falls). This Qingdao facility is an exciting project, a tremendous educational and tourist attraction for China, and a scientifically important biological environment.

To get the best results, you need to place your indoor water fountain in the right place. Choose southwest for a new partner, southeast for good luck and prosperity, and to further your career, go for the north.

When you make your own water fountain, you can beautify it in many personal ways: candles and flowers, lighting, and mirrors can all enhance your water feature.

YOUR FAMILY TREE

The Chinese have a reputation for looking after their elders, and they have a long history of ancestor searches. They have recorded their findings for nearly 1000 years, so if you happen to have Chinese heritage, modern research into your Chinese family can be very satisfying.

A zupu (also called a jaipu) is a Chinese genealogy book recording the lineage and famous members of a family.

But many countries maintain similar records; for example, births and deaths are recorded in the church registers, land changes in the title office, and people wrote about their personal journeys and kept diaries.

I remember a friend showing me around Hereford, UK, and pointing out the market cross, where her ancestor had been hanged for disorderly behavior.

You never know what you will turn up!

What Chinese Genealogy Records Exist?

Before paper was invented, records were kept on shells, bones, and bronze in the early days. People sometimes tied small objects into knots in ropes to keep in touch with previous generations.

Jaipu were the manuscripts used from around the 1600s. Even poor people revered their ancestors and kept their own jaipu. Many of these survive to this day; some are scattered, and others published, but many were destroyed in the cultural revolution of the 1960s and 1970s.

Inside the jaipu, people may find information about migration, military, and government affairs as well as praise of the worthy and encouragement for future generations to bring honor to the family.

While reasonably complete records of the males are often found, daughters might be left out, as are relatives who had shamed the family or entered a monastery.

And just in case you are wondering whether you have any famous ancestors, think about this: Genghis Khan, a mighty and victorious Mongolian warrior in the 13th century, not only conquered and ruled the largest empire in the world, but he also helped to populate the world. He has about 16 million descendants alive today!

If you decide that you would like to know more about your ancestors, there are many places you can go for help on the internet. In addition, you can buy albums to record your information and make your own jaipu.

PAPERMAKING

The Chinese invented papermaking. A Chinese court official named Cai Lun has gained credit for the invention of papermaking, although it was probably around before him. But he did introduce the idea of sheets of paper sometime around the year 105 CE.

Previously, people wrote on silken cloth, but that has its own problems and was expensive as well. Cai discovered a cheaper alternative that gave a smoother writing surface. He used hemp waste, old rags, fishnets, and the bark of trees.

From China, the papermaking sills were exported to Korea and then to Japan by Buddhist monks around 610 CE.

Nowadays, you don't have to go hunting around for old rags and the bark of trees – you can buy kits to make your own paper at home. And when you have produced your beautiful paper, you will have many uses for your paper, including handwriting your own words.

CALLIGRAPHY

Chinese calligraphy is an art form, widely practiced and respected. In ancient China, the four most sought-after skills and hobbies were:

- The board game "Go" (a simple concept but an incredibly cunning game)
- Playing a stringed instrument
- Painting (which is allied to calligraphy)

- Calligraphy itself

One could go a stage further. China is expansive and could only be ruled with the help of a massive civil service. The only female empress, empress Wu Zetian, declared that entry into this prestigious service required one to write poetry – and it was a stiff test.

Chinese characters were being written as long ago as 4000 BCE on ceramics with cinnabar paint. The characters were also inscribed on ox shoulder blades and tortoise shells, possibly used as oracle bones to foretell the future.

What distinguishes Chinese calligraphy?

There is an emphasis on motion: the writing is dynamic and seems to be moving. The time and rhythm are emphasized and offset by the use of white space.

After fountain pens came to China from the West and italic writing became popular, traditional Chinese calligraphy was used less and less. The italic script originated in the Pope's office because it is elegant and, importantly, legible. Just like the Chinese characters, the spacing and proportions of hand-written italic writing are an art.

Now we have computers, and the use of italic writing for emphasis and quotations has become so easy that it can seem a chore to hand-write anything, especially calligraphy; but the art of beautiful writing still enthuses many people worldwide. It's relaxing as you take the time to focus on each letter, as every one has to be perfect.

Calligraphy is decorative, but there are formal rules, and you need very few tools to get started.

You'll need a brush, ink stick, inkstone, and special mulberry paper to create this beautiful art. As you practice and gain confidence, your work will become more fluid and beautiful.

TAI CHI

Like so many Chinese hobbies, tai chi has a spiritual as well as a practical outlet.

It is a gentle form of slow, dance-like exercise. It is perfect for any age group, and the older person can do this without strain or stress on their bodies.

The movements are slow, your muscles are gently stretched, and your breathing deepens. You focus on the feeling of the movements as your body flows from one movement to the next without pause. Your body constantly moves but at your own pace.

You don't need special equipment. You don't need classes or company, although you will see people of all ages moving together in China, outside, in parks and squares. But you can do this on your balcony, in your garden, or any place where you feel comfortable.

The fact that tai chi is low impact makes it suitable for people who need to move without putting pressure on aching joints, and it does make a calm and refreshing start to a day.

You can practice your mindfulness if you wish, or enjoy the sky and the trees and perhaps the birds singing, just for you.

SUMMARY

From feng shui to indoor waterfalls, the Chinese have made the creation of their indoor environments into an art. Practical, physical ways to enhance the space you live in are combined with patience and respect for your inner mind.

Many of us are interested in our ancestors, none more than the Chinese. Making your own family trees can throw up some unexpected discoveries.

For an extraordinary craft item, you could make your own paper and use your best calligraphy pen to write a charming poem.

Relaxing your body as well as your mind. Tai chi is gentle, controlled, and calming – something most of us need in our busy lives. China has so much to offer.

>   Feng shui
>   Indoor waterfalls
>   Family trees
>   Papermaking
>   Calligraphy
>   Tai chi

THE NETHERLANDS

The Netherlands is a fantastic place. Nearly a quarter of its territory is below sea level, including the Schiphol international airport. But the Netherlands defenses are worthy of respect: a network of dams and storm barriers to protect this low-lying country from rising sea levels.

The iconic windmills, the tulip fields full of color, the clogs, and the cheese markets make this a special place. In addition, there are the craftspeople who produce the renowned Delft Blue earthenware and the famous Flemish old masters. And everywhere you go, there are bicycles – millions of them – for the country is flat.

So, let's explore a few of the hobbies you can find in the Netherlands.

ICE SKATING

The English word skate is derived from the Dutch word "Schaats," and ice skating in the Netherlands can be traced to 800 CE. Although, originally, the skate may have been made from animal bones. Many years later, wood was substituted for bone, and the first iron skates were made in the 1500s.

The weather used to be colder, and every winter, the waterways iced over, so skating was a practical form of transport for people and goods.

Nowadays, when the canals ice over and the skates come out, it's time to enjoy the speed and freedom of skating, plus the change in scenery that snow and ice give the landscape. Along with kiosks that sell hot drinks and snacks, ice skating is widespread, and any age can participate. In the Netherlands, thousands come out to play when the ice is firm.

The linking of skating with "koek and zopie" (cookies and hooch) goes back to the 17th century when this magical drink was created—an alcoholic and spicy concoction that includes beer, rum, cinnamon, and eggs. Now sadly, it's mostly split pea soup and hot chocolate that is served.

For those intrigued, here is a typical recipe for zopie:

3 12 oz bottles of a dark beer
1 cinnamon stick
2 cloves, whole
2 slices of lemon
1 cup brown sugar
2 eggs
4 Tbsp rum

Bring the dark beer, with the cinnamon stick, cloves, and lemon slices to a boil, then turn the heat down and simmer for about fifteen minutes. Whip the brown sugar with the eggs until foamy.

Carefully add a Tbsp of warm beer to the egg mixture and stir. Do this five more times, then take the beer off the stove. Remove the cinnamon stick, lemon, and cloves. Carefully stir the rest of the beer into the eggs in a tiny stream. Make sure the eggs don't curdle and keep stirring. Pour everything back in the pan, and return the pan to the heat, but do not let the mixture boil, just warm it up and keep stirring until the beverage thickens a bit and it looks smooth and velvety in texture.

All that is left is to stir in the rum, add some whipped cream, and a pinch of cinnamon!

The Netherlands dominates speed skating in the Olympic games, and the Dutch have won around 25% of the medals since 1924 – especially impressive given that the Netherlands is a small country.

Sadly, with the climate warming up, the skating season in the Netherlands is getting shorter and shorter. This sport has to wait for safe conditions, and you can't just take the skates out as soon as the canals freeze over. A thickness of almost three inches of ice is generally deemed safe but local conditions may vary, and people do drown every year when they fail to check.

But if your area reaches low temperatures, there is nothing quite so exhilarating as ice skating, and many areas either have indoor ice rinks all year-round or make them as the winter temperature drops. You can sometimes find them as part of the Christmas markets.

A word of caution, though, as old bones can break more easily than young ones, so don't go trying to out-speed the youth – let them win sometimes! But taken gently and with care, ice skating can be an excellent hobby for those winter days when it can be tempting to laze by the fire or under the blankets.

CHEESEMAKING

Most countries have their own famous and favorite cheeses, and the Netherlands is no exception.

With its characteristic red rind, Edam has been exported to many corners of the world for hundreds of years. You can visit the town of Edam and explore the cheese warehouses of the 1700s. Millions of tons of cheese are exported every year. And just 50 miles away is the home of Gouda, another, slightly more decadent cheese.

The cheeses are made with milk – although there are now vegan options available. Gouda uses whole-fat dairy, and Edam is made from lower-fat dairy, so it tastes slightly drier.

In the Netherlands, wooden vessels were traditionally used to manufacture cheese since metals were not locally available. They had to heat these by adding hot water as fire would burn them. To make room for the water, as much whey was removed as possible; we now call this method the "washed curd" method of cheese making. This gives the cheese its unique flavor. The cheese tends to be milder and sweeter than many other kinds of cheese.

About ten liters of milk are needed to make one kilo of Gouda cheese. First, the milk is pasteurized, and then a small amount of culture is added, followed by liquid rennet, then annatto for color.

The Netherlands has special "cheese markets," with a great variety of delicious cheeses on show. But how about making your own cheese?

There are many workshops on the internet, plus books, courses, and videos on making the perfect cheese. However, if you make your own Gouda, it usually takes about six weeks before you can taste the finished product.

There are kits with everything (including instructions) supplied, and there are vegan kits as well. So you might be able to show off your own cheese at your wine and cheese tasting sessions or simply enjoy your creations yourself.

FLOWER GROWING AND ARRANGING

The Netherlands is famous for its tulips – fields, and fields of them in the spring, full of color and depth – one of the most fabulous flower shows on earth.

Tulips came to Europe from the Far East via the spice trading routes; they were deemed exotic, and it was "bad taste" for any wealthy man to be without his own tulip collection.

The golden age for Dutch tulips was in the mid-17th century, when "tulip mania" was in season. The price of tulips was beyond that of gold. The rarest bulbs were priced at six times an average salary, or 10,000 guilders (for which you could buy a fine mansion on the Grand Canal in Amsterdam).

Of course, the inevitable happened, and the tulip market bubble crashed – one of the most spectacular market crashes of all time.

The Dutch not only produce the finest tulips, but they also know how to create some of the most innovative and exciting flower arrangements you can find anywhere. Dutch floral designers travel worldwide to demonstrate their skills, and people from many countries travel to the Netherlands to study the art of flower arranging. There are trade fairs, exhibitions, and courses available for the keen florist.

The delight of flower arranging is that you can use any flowers and greenery available to you – even the daisies on your lawn – to make lovely arrangements to beautify your home or to give as gifts.

Naturally, one has to be careful not to over-pick the flowers: in some areas, picking wildflowers is forbidden to preserve their beauty for future generations. But, on the other hand, buying flowers in season is not expensive.

Not only do the arrangements look pretty, but you also get a sense of peace and tranquility when putting them together, and, depending on how seriously you take up this hobby, you need very little in the way of equipment.

All you need is a good pair of sharp floral clippers and perhaps floral netting, tape, or sponge. To preserve your creation, try adding one teaspoon of sugar to one liter of water.

SUMMARY

Think of the Netherlands, and the image of tulips springs to mind. Flower power is very real here. But growing and arranging flowers is a hobby for anyone.

The Dutch people shine at speed skating, and when the canals freeze over in winter, out come the skates. Speed skating might not be for you, but ice rinks open up in winter, and you could have a good laugh learning how to skate.

One of the other things the Netherlands is renowned for is its cheese, and cheese making is a Netherland hobby you could copy. Many countries have their own cheeses, so it might be worth finding out about the cheese in your part of the world. If you like cheese, then this is a hobby for you.

> Ice skating
> Cheesemaking
> Flower growing and arranging

I hope that the wheels are turning and you are thinking of ways to enjoy life to its fullest by starting new creative hobbies. I wrote this book for people just like you and me, transitioning into retirement or already into your golden years.

As a Health & Life Coach, it is important not to leave anyone out. Everyone deserves to live a vibrant life, so if this book has brought you some joy, a glimmer of hope, or a solid plan to improve upon your day-to-day, I have a favor to ask you. Please stop what you are doing right now, and go to your computer or phone and leave a review on your Amazon account or wherever you purchased this book.

Your review will greatly help other readers decide if this book is for them. Thank you for taking the time to leave a review.

BRAZIL

Brazil is immense: it takes up nearly half the continent of South America. Renowned for coffee, carnivals, and costumes, Brazil has unrivaled beaches and an energetic, party-like atmosphere.

Alongside the atmosphere of an urban festival are over 1,300,000 square miles of Amazon jungle. The Amazon is crucial to our planet, with its 390 billion trees producing a sizable fraction of our world's oxygen supply, as well as providing a home for an extraordinary amount of biodiversity. Roughly 60% of the world's rainforest is situated in Brazil, although at the moment, it is decreasing every day.

We have not yet plumbed the depths of the treasure to be found in the wild forests of Brazil, which may one day provide insights into new medicinal drugs, ecological systems, and a treasure trove of undiscovered flora and fauna.

Brazil offers a wide diversity of scenery and architecture. Life there is vibrant and energetic, never more so than dancing the samba, their traditional dance. While Portuguese is the official language, illustrating Brazil's colonial history, tribes we have never met may still be living in isolation in the forests.

There is much to discover – and much to enjoy – so let's have a look at some of the hobbies you can find in Brazil.

CARNAVAL DO BRASIL

Nowhere does carnival quite like Brazil!

Every year, the streets are filled with dancing people in fantastic and colorful costumes. Around two million people fill the streets, and the economy benefits from 500,000 visitors. It's one gigantic party.

If you have the chance, visit the Brazil carnival for a once-in-a-lifetime experience.

But even if that is not possible, there are often carnivals in many towns and villages throughout the world, and you can take part.

The floats take time to prepare, the costumes need designing, making, and altering, the band's practice marching, ideas flow, and everyone who participates is part of the team. Often the tractors or wagons need to be in perfect order; no one wants to be stranded in the middle of the parade. There are work or volunteer jobs suitable for everyone.

The noise, the excitement, the route lined with spectators – even if it isn't in Brazil, it can be exhilarating, and usually, anyone who can help, even in a small way, is very welcome indeed.

Taking part in the preparations for your local carnival can be pretty exhausting as the day draws nearer and nearer, but it is a great way to be part of your local community. And the kids love it.

It might be a time to practice your samba just like they dance it on the streets of Brazil.

SAMBA

The samba is the traditional national dance in Brazil. Brazilians dance it at carnivals and everywhere else they go.

The samba is a mixture of African drumming and European marches. The origins are rooted in the colonial slave culture: the Africans brought dance, music, and drums.

But the samba is a happy, lively, and upbeat dance. It has a rolling hip action, pelvic tilt, and a bouncy rhythm. You need to be supple to move your torso and give expression to the dance. But most of all, the samba is fun!

The dance costume varies, but the emphasis is on the elaborate headpiece allied with a bikini-style outfit or a long, flowing skirt and wrap-tie top.

Elements of rock and jazz have updated the samba, so it really is a dance for everyone.

If there are classes near you, then you are fortunate. If not, there are videos on the internet, and maybe you could persuade others to join you?

Samba is all about joy and passion. The movements are fast, but no one is watching the meticulous, well-ordered sequences – you can do it your way. And if you are a little stiff, you can move any way that suits you.

There is no need to overdo the action – just relax and enjoy the lively music and the movements you can comfortably make, even if that is only tapping your foot and watching from the sidelines.

CHEESE BREAD MAKING

Pão de queijo, otherwise known as cheese bread, is found everywhere you go in Brazil, and it is delicious and straightforward to prepare.

The cheese bread is made from cassava flour and Brazilian cheese. Don't worry if they are not in your local supermarket – substitutions are acceptable, and you can experiment to find your favorite flours and cheeses.

You can eat this anytime, but in Brazil, breakfast is often chosen as the best time to enjoy Pão de queijo. It's definitely something to get up for.

Here is a recipe you can make with ingredients from your local grocery store.

The results are soft, gooey, and very cheesy rolls. You can even freeze them.

Ingredients

- 4 cups tapioca flour
- 1/2 cup water
- 1 1/4 cups milk
- 2 large eggs
- 6 tablespoons oil
- 1 cup shredded mozzarella cheese
- 1 1/2 cups grated parmesan cheese

- 2 teaspoons salt

Instructions

- Preheat the oven to 400°F.
- Combine the milk, water, oil, and salt in a saucepan to boil over medium-high heat.
- Put the tapioca flour into the bowl of a mixer and, when the milk mix boils, pour it over the flour.
- Mix it well. It will come out white and sticky.
- With the mixer still on, add eggs, one at a time.
- Then add the cheese, a little at a time, until thoroughly mixed in.
- The dough is supposed to be soft and sticky. Add a little more flour if necessary – but not too much.
- Shape dough into balls by wetting your hands with cold water, make balls slightly smaller than golf balls.
- Place balls on baking sheet. Cover with parchment paper.
- Bake 15 to 20 minutes or until golden and puffed.

Try not to eat them all at once!

ARMCHAIR CAVING

Many countries have amazing caverns and caves – and I am not suggesting you don protective gear, oxygen tanks and descend deep into the earth's crust. Caving can be a dangerous sport and is best left to the young, supple, and expert.

However, the earth is riddled with holes of various kinds, and learning about them, perhaps making a journal about them, will lead you to find out many fascinating facts about our planet. Why leave it all to the youth? Let them do the hard work, and you can enjoy the knowledge gained.

You can explore the underground town of Derinkuyu in Turkey, where over 20,000 people once lived. You can marvel at the 30,000-year-old images of horses and bison skillfully painted on the walls of caves like Lascaux in France. You could dive deep into caves in Yucatán, explore ancient cities like Herculaneum, and you can delve deep into caves with small entrances without brushing against the giant spiders that lurk there near the entrance.

But one of the best places in the world to find "paleo burrows" is Brazil. So, to start your journal, here are a few facts about paleo burrows:

In 2008, Heinrich Frank was driving along a Brazilian highway when he noticed a strange-looking hole by the side of the road. Frank was a geologist, and he had never seen anything like this before, so he explored further.

The tunnel was elliptical and around three feet in diameter. On the walls were deep gash marks – like the claw marks of a large animal. Water could not have made this tunnel. Neither could tectonic activity or lava flows. It had to be made by an animal, and a large animal at that.

It is believed that giant sloths were at work here. Although they became extinct 10,000 years ago, they have left their mark. In fact, Frank went on to discover over 1500 paleo burrows in Brazil.

There are so many more fascinating facts to find out about in exploring our underground caverns, and you can do it all from an armchair. The internet is full of incredible cave images and videos.

However, if you get the opportunity to descend into a cave as part of a guided group, it is an experience like no other, and the experience will stay with you forever.

SUMMARY

The country of Brazil is enormous, and Brazilians know how to party. Their carnivals are possibly the best in the world for extravagant costumes and lively progressions. You can watch the genuine article or join your local carnival committee – both are fun things to do.

The samba reflects the lively nature of the Brazilian people, but you don't have to compete with them when you have your own little samba session – you have the freedom to dance how you feel.

When you need a break, make some cheese bread – it's delicious any time. And armchair caving can take you places you would never, ever explore yourself, but you can still enjoy the beauty of the underground world.

>Carnival
>Samba
>Cheese bread making
>Armchair caving

PORTUGAL

Do you know that half of the New World once belonged to Portugal? The Treaty of Tordesillas was signed in 1495. This divided the New World between Spain and Portugal,

Portugal having the eastern half. The treaty was in effect for 300 years, and Portuguese is still the national language of Brazil.

Portugal has a rich maritime history. Many famous explorers were Portuguese – sailors like Vasco da Gama (1460 - 1524) and Ferdinand Magellan (1480 - 1521), after whom the famous Magellan Straits around the southern tip of South America is named.

In many ways, Portugal is a relaxed country – the dances are less fierce than in neighboring Spain. Time-keeping can be elastic, and people tend to be tolerant and patient.

But their all-consuming passion, like in so many other countries, is football! Futebol, the beautiful game, has followers in every town, and perhaps the world's best player, Cristiano Ronaldo, is Portuguese. So it's not hard to start a conversation about football.

But crafts like embroidery and lace-making are popular, and so are water sports and their own traditional dancing.

FANDANGO AND FADO

Portuguese folk dancing illustrates courtship and marriage as well as local customs for each region. The dances are controlled and require practice and stamina to perform well. They are usually slower in pace than those of Spain. Famous dances include the fandango, chula, vira, and veranda.

Fado is the main music and song of Portugal. The tunes and lyrics are often sad and melancholy, but they do have an important traditional role. Fado is on UNESCO's "Representative List of the Intangible Cultural Heritage of Humanity." It is often played without dancing nowadays and offers a tiny peep at the past lives of poor and seafaring folk.

The pace of the dancing suits mature people and is a lovely way to spend an evening. Learning to fandango could be a relaxing, somewhat nostalgic hobby. You would need to find a group for the best experience, but there are online courses for you to pass a few hours in peace and tranquility in your own home.

There is a free online app called FandangoNOW that you can install onto your tablet or iOS. Why not try it and see?

BOBBIN LACE-MAKING

Portugal is renowned for its needlework crafts, embroidery, and lace-making. There are many craft fairs where you can examine and admire the gorgeous handiwork.

Lace-making has a history going back to at least 1616. It created a vital income for the area of Vila do Conde, but King João tried to ban lace from the ordinary people. The local lace makers were outraged and forced the king to withdraw his ban.

But the introduction of industrial lace-making in the 20th century forced a reduction in the home lace-making industry. As a result, the number of lace-makers declined from more than 500 to a mere 100 since the 1940s.

However, home lace-making was rescued by the introduction of annual fairs, handicraft centers, and contests. Lace-making it now alive and well in Portugal. There is even a statue of a bobbin lace maker in Vila de Conde, situated on the quay to commemorate those industrious ladies who made lace while their husbands were at sea. Yet another sculpture can be found in the fishing town Peniche, together with a museum dedicated to the craft of bobbin lace-making.

While lace-making is a skill, it can be learned, and lace-makers are often keen to share their knowledge. You may be lucky enough to find a group near you, which could be great for socializing as you craft a beautiful piece of lace. And lace is versatile and is not just for doilies, collars, and tableware; how about a lovely, lacy curtain to diffuse the sunlight? And, perhaps best of all, a lacy wedding dress?

How about starting your own lace-making group?

EMBROIDERY

Portuguese crafts are not confined to lace-making; their embroidery is also much sought after, and there are also expert knitters, crocheters, and rug makers.

Traditionally, their craftwork started in the nunneries and then as cottage industries to provide extra income for the fisher families and farmers. Each region has its own unique style.

Portuguese embroidery is rich in color and may involve a vast number of intricate stitches. White embroidery – using white thread on white cloth – is also popular now.

This hobby is another excellent opportunity for socializing. Still, it can just as equally be carried on at home, in the garden, or snug by the fireside on a cold winter's evening. And there are many books to give you ideas and instructions.

Embroidery can be a way to liven up an inexpensive blouse and make it something rather special. It can also be used to make jewelry, tableware, and gifts of all kinds.

CANOEING AND KAYAKING

With the coastline never far away, it's natural that windsurfing, kite surfing, and sailing are all popular. In fact, the largest wave ever surfed was recorded about 30 minutes north of Peniche.

But if you do not live near the coast, canoeing can be carried out on rivers as well as the sea. Canoeing is a popular sport both for the tourists and the locals in Portugal, and they have many top Olympians in canoeing and kayaking.

Less expensive than owning a boat, a canoe can be parked in the garage or hallway and brought out when you feel the need for some peace and quiet, a few moments of precious time for reflection, and even a workout – you might be surprised how much energy your legs burn; it's not just arm work.

Much of the kayaking in Portugal is done in two- or even three-seater kayak and is very safe. It is also a fantastic way to explore places that would otherwise be inaccessible.

It's a good idea to learn from an expert how to escape if your kayak turns over, which it will. The kayak roll is easy to master for a single-seater and could save you from a few very unpleasant moments.

PAINTBALL

Paintball is popular in Portugal. The country has several large paintball parks, and you probably have one near you as well, since this is a sport for all worldwide.

In Portugal, they have paintball parks in the open countryside, and the game is suitable for anyone over the age of ten and in reasonably good health. Very often, you play in teams.

Paintball uses guns that fire not bullets but balls of paint. This clearly shows where you have been hit. Cheating is not an option!

Strategy is all. Flanking maneuvers, duels, and retreats all play a part. The park will provide the equipment you need – markers, vests, color balls, as well as protective gear as required.

If the paintball park is good, there will be plenty of room for strategy; it's not just a game for the fastest and fittest. But this is something you can do with your grandchildren – they might have the energy, but you have the brains.

SUMMARY

The people of Portugal have a relaxed way of life, which is reflected in their traditional dances such as the fandango and their evocative music, the fado. The pace of the dances and music suit mature people who like to take their time and make the most of the pleasure.

But in active sports, the Portuguese excel in canoeing and kayaking, which is surprisingly energetic. It's a fine way to keep fit, and if there is a class near you, they will teach you how to get out of the upturned kayak with ease.

Another energetic activity for all ages (usually over the age of ten) is paintball; if you haven't tried it yet, that is a treat in store.

Portugal is famous for its beautiful lace and delicate embroidery. These crafts can be pursued at home alone and in friendly groups to catch up on all the local news.

>
> Fandango and fado
> Bobbin lace-making
> Embroidery
> Canoeing and Kayaking
> Paintball

FIJI

Composed of over 300 islands in the South Pacific, Fiji enjoys a tropical climate and stunning scenery.

In the days of sailing ships, sailors tended to avoid Fiji, partly because of the treacherous waters but also because the inhabitants fiercely defended their territory. The men carved weapons, canoes, and knew how to use them.

But now, the tourist trade is the primary money earner, and many of the traditions continue to entice visitors. Grass skirts, war paint, and garlands of colorful flowers might greet the traveler. Even the treacherous waters are popular, some of the best waves for surfing are located near Fiji. The famous "Cloudbreaker" – an 18-foot wave, attracts surfers from afar.

Over the ground and under the sea, the scenery is spectacular. Many of the islands are tiny but packed with streams and waterfalls. The tropical jungle, the blue skies, and the coastal vistas make Fiji truly an enchanting place.

NATURE TRAILS AND GUIDED WALKS

The nature trails in Fiji are stunning. Fiji isn't just coral reefs and sandy beaches: there is a wealth of stunning scenery inland (although you are never far from the sea). Fiji's largest island, Viti Levu, has mountains, with Mount Tomanivi rising to 4,344 ft. Throughout the islands, there are nature trails to show off the very best areas and to allow you to meet the varied wildlife.

One example is the Lavena Coastal Walk. This three-hour hike takes in a coastline of black volcanic sandy beaches, rocky cliffs, waterfalls, and a village (where good manners mean you must wait to be invited in). The final waterfall can only be reached by swimming, so you might need a guide.

There are guided walks in most parts of the world, from ghost-spotting walks in London to a hike down the Parisian catacombs to "proper" nature trails. What is there on offer near you?

If you are like most of us, you may have traveled to far-off places to see their sights but may not have explored your local terrain. It might be worth seeing what is available closer to home.

You might even consider becoming a qualified guide to take others on a nature ramble or sightseeing around a historic building; volunteers are always needed. It is very satisfying to share your love and knowledge of places with other people.

LOVO – COOKING UNDERGROUND

An earth oven is one of the easiest and oldest methods of cooking. Little equipment is required, and if the power goes out, you can still produce a fabulous meal with just a fire to heat the stones and a hole in the ground.

Traditional cooking underground is huge in Fiji: families and restaurants all cook fish, chicken, and vegetables in improvised underground ovens. The result is succulent and delicious. Lovo is often the centerpiece of celebrations, weddings, and festivals. Fijians are experts in socializing, partying, and having a great time.

In Fiji, families will make a shallow hole in the ground and place heated stones at the base. Coconut husks are then used to line the oven. Palm leaves go on top of the hot stones, and this is followed by the vegetables, chicken, and breadfruit wrapped in more leaves and coconut fronds. This is covered with the soil and left to cook on its own for about an hour or maybe more. You can cook a huge amount of food at the same time with no risk of burning or overcooking. Just add sauces made from Polynesian fruit, chillis, and spices, and you can create your own Fijian feast.

Some of the restaurants use elaborate braiding of the banana leaves to enclose the food, and after being decorated with flowers, the results look and smell tantalizingly attractive.

Dessert can be cooked alongside the main course; for example, egg custard or vakalolo – which is coconut and cassava – steamed till soft and served with caramel sauce.

Just as in our more familiar barbecues, it's typically the men who prepare the lovo.

And there is no reason why you can't make your own lovo as long as you have access to a small piece of ground (and a shovel.)

Here's how to make your own earth oven:

Find a suitable place – one where there is no fire hazard.

1. Create a hole about two by three feet and a foot deep – keep the sides as vertical as possible.
2. Line the bottom and sides with flattish rocks. (If the stones are rounded, you may need a slightly bigger pit.)
3. Time to build a small fire to heat the rocks. Allow to burn for 45 minutes to an hour before it dies down.

Do not use wet or waterlogged stones, as the water trapped inside them might explode in the heat.

Your oven is prepared; now to put in the food, and if you do not have banana fronds and palm leaves, you can use tinfoil. Cover with the earth you have removed, and wait patiently or have a go at Fijian dancing to stimulate your appetite.

CRICKET

Cricket probably originated as a children's game in southeast England during the 13th century. They used a stone as a ball and a branch from the dense forest surrounding them at that time as the bat.

The game evolved: balls were no longer stone, and bats changed from a curved shape to a straight and wider one, often made from willow tree wood.

In the 19th century, English sailors carried their love of cricket to faraway places, including Fiji, where it is still a popular pastime today.

Fiji now has a men's team to play in the International Cricket Council (ICC) matches.

Although football is becoming increasingly popular, cricket still has a place in the hearts of many. Since it involves less physical contact than many other sports, it is suitable for all ages. But the masks and the hard balls and aggressive playing of some members can make this a risky game.

There is a saying, "It's just not cricket," which roughly means, "It's not fair," or "It's not the done thing."

You may prefer to play "French Cricket." This family game involves all members of the family playing at the same time, so there are no long periods of sitting out, waiting for your turn to bat.

SUMMARY

Fiji might not be very big, but the numerous islands possess incredible natural beauty, which, together with the generous and welcoming population, makes them an excellent tourist venue.

The activities in Fiji are as varied as the scenery, and many of them are great tourist attractions as well. Becoming a walking guide, lovo cooking underground, or taking up cricket are all hobbies you can pursue in your own country,

       Nature trails and Guided Walks
       Lovo underground cooking
       Cricket

THE GAMBIA

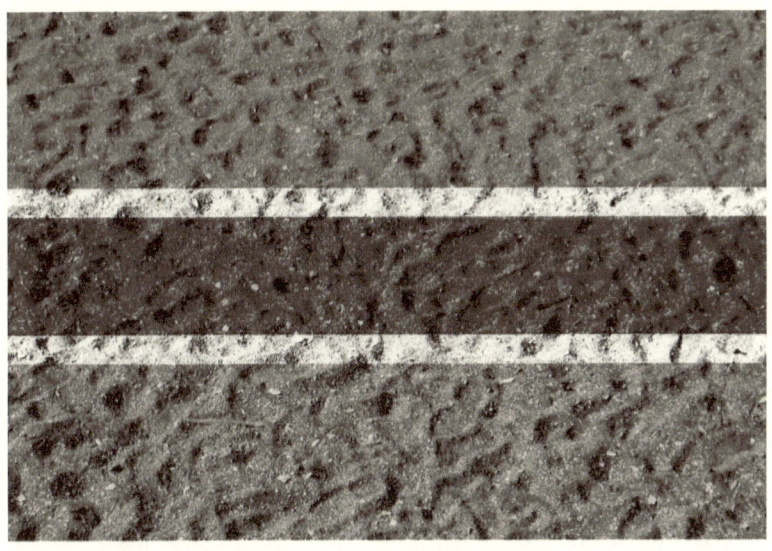

The Republic of Gambia is the smallest country in Africa, but it is bursting with natural beauty, culture, and history.

A thin stretch of land only 30 miles wide, it borders the Gambia river, and is surrounded by the country of Senegal. One of the world's poorest countries, the Gambia used to be a center for the slave trade, and vestiges of that time still remain.

Today, the most significant industry is tourism. Gambians are proud of their country, and tourists will often end up with a young man to guide them to the markets and other places of interest. The markets are full of color, and sunhats, dresses, shirts, and wooden carvings of animals are all on display, plus so much more.

For the bird watcher, The Gambia is paradise. You can also visit a crocodile center and even stroke a croc if you are brave enough (they are well fed, so it is claimed they are not dangerous).

The 50 miles of scenic coastline allows one to relax in the sunshine, swim in warm waters, and generally chill out. So what hobbies do they have in The Gambia?

WOOD CARVING

Wood carving might be a hobby, but it is also a source of income. Every piece is unique – all hand-carved from local wood such as bombax, silk cotton, or mahogany.

Favorite items are local animals – antelope, crocodiles, giraffes, lions, elephants, monkeys, and turtles. But household objects such as bowls and dishes, musical instruments such as the balafon (a kind of wooden xylophone), and the local djembe drum are also commonly carved.

The method of carving has been handed down through the generations. First, a chunk of wood is chosen. Then the work starts using tools for deep cuts, with finer details added after the main shape has been created. Carving is never against the grain of the wood. Finally, the items are finished off with a coat of oil – linseed or walnut – to give a shiny, smooth finish that catches the light.

Wood carving is a hobby you could take up, although you are unlikely to reach the standard of these traditional Gambian carvings without a lot of practice. Choose a locally available softwood to start, attend a class, and be prepared for a steep learning curve.

But whittling away has always been something people loved to do while passing a few hours of time. You could improve on that and actually produce your own Gambian-style crocodile with a kink in its tail or a salad bowl that has a unique and endearing shape.

DRUMMING

In The Gambia, you can hear and see the djembe drums (pronounced "jem-bay") everywhere. They are an integral part of life, performing at weddings, births, and funerals, or just jamming on the beach for the delight of it.

The drums are constructed with great skill since the body is made from a single tree trunk, using those renowned Gambian carving skills, and the drum head is made from goatskin. The skin is made taut by tightening ropes around the body of the drum to tune it. Then, it is played with bare hands.

The djembe may have been in use as long ago as the 12th century. The name derives from words meaning "all gather together in peace," and this drum is not one used in war. With a little bit of practice, a djembe can produce many different sounds, and the player can tell an emotional story with this drum.

Djembes are not large drums – a medium-sized one might weigh about 20 lb – and by tradition, they are played by men. Women often play accompanying instruments, such as a kese kese, a kind of rattle.

The people of The Gambia grow up with the rhythm of the djembe, and when a group plays together, each may play their own individual tune, which interlocks to form a whole. At times, the melodies merge to form a united pattern and then diverge again to go their separate ways. It can be very complex and sometimes quite hard to follow for one unused to it.

Drumming makes a great hobby, especially if you are new to learning a musical instrument. It doesn't have to be complex, and it isn't hard to get an acceptable sound. You can play in a group or all on your own, but feeling the rhythm beating inside you as you drum can be intoxicating. Just remember that sound travels, and these drums were sometimes used to carry messages long distances.

SUMMARY

The Gambia is a small, poor country but is brimming with vitality. The carved animals are attractive and very collectible. It would be an interesting challenge for you to produce your own wood carving of an equal standard.

Gambians also make their own drums, and drumming is a marvelous way to let off steam. Their djembe drums can be found in many countries. Drumming is an easy way to enjoy performing regardless of your starting level of musical talent, using different types of drums for very different sounds.

      Wood carving
      Drumming

AUSTRALIA

A ustralia is BIG. It has both the vigor of new blood and some of the oldest traditions in the world.

This mix is recognized and celebrated, but conflicts between new arrivals and the Indigenous population have left their mark. The English penal colonies could be places of brutality, yet also gave opportunities to those able and lucky enough to benefit from them. We have wonderful artists, craftsmen, and great statesmen who emerged from those dark prisons.

The rugged landscape of vast, arid deserts has shaped many of the activities of the people who live there. There are also forests – now subject to fire as the climate heats up – impressive coral reefs, which are also in danger from warmer seas; the challenges are enormous. Still, the vitality of the people seems undaunted.

What follows is just a small selection of the hobbies Australians enjoy.

ROCK ART AND PEBBLE PAINTING

According to a book by Ian Wilson, "Lost World of the Kimberley," rock art in Australia may go back as far as 50,000 years. He describes Northwest Australia as a vast, arid, boulder-strewn place with hundreds of rock shelters, many with signs of paintings.

But the findings are confusing since the aboriginal people continue to paint the rocks, and they have a deeply religious significance. It isn't easy to be sure of how old the artwork is, even with technologies like carbon dating.

However a recent finding, a painting of a kangaroo, has been dated as 17,300 years old. The painting is 6'5" inches long and painted with red ochre on the roof of a rock shelter in Kimberley, in Western Australia.

But other findings suggest that rock art goes back further in Australia. In ancient times, travellers to Australia from Asia needed shorter sea trips than today, since the sea has risen, covering many of the smaller island stops in between.

The Kimberley kangaroo painting is remarkably similar to rock paintings in Southeast Asia, which have been dated to over 40,000 years old. So this does suggest a link. In Indonesia, the earliest animal painting we know of is a life-size depiction of a pig, which is 45,000 years old. But the oldest painting of all is a doodle in South Africa, dated 73,000 years ago.

In modern times, we have taken to painting pebbles and stones instead of caves. Rock or pebble painting needs nothing more than a decent rock, a lick of paint, and perhaps a coat of varnish to keep it looking nice. You may want to stick a piece of soft cloth underneath your finished pebble to protect any surface you put it on.

These painted pebbles make ingenious paperweights, or door stops, or just interesting ornaments. It's a hobby you can share with grandchildren – hunting for the right pebble is an integral part of the procedure, and kids are good at this.

You may wish to hide them in local parks, inviting people to photograph them and post them on social media. Recently, an artist painted pebbles depicting the Olympic winners.

Your own imagination is the only limit on how you create and use these modern rock paintings.

WATERCOLORS

Between 1804 and 1853, Britain transported roughly 76,000 convicts to Tasmania.

Some of these convicts were industrious; others were talented artists. Their works are not only beautiful to look at but are also of considerable historical interest. Photography was only beginning to be developed. These artists ranged from the habitually drunk but very talented, to the well-behaved model prisoner.

William Gould was very talented, when sober.

He was transported to Australia for stealing a coat, and during the voyage, he painted the officers' portraits. Once in Tasmania, he continued his way of petty crime, including the forgery of banknotes. He ended up working for a doctor/naturalist and painted fish, birds, and plants. Once freed, he continued to drink, and the high standard of his best work declined. But Gould's original Sketchbook of Fishes was of world significance, depicting some fish that are now extinct.

Then there was Thomas Bock, the "best portrait painter of them all." He was transported to Australia for giving his mistress drugs to induce an abortion. His job was preparing plates for banknotes! But his portraits, especially of young infants who had died, were sensitive and empathic.

Once free, he became interested in early photography and created beautiful portraits of the Indigenous people and the colonists – another valuable insight into the conditions of life among the early colonists and convicts.

Some of the convict paintings are a delight to gaze at, but they also offer a historical value. There were many more convict artists – but you don't need to be in prison to paint.

Watercolor painting is a beautiful way to pass your time and produce unique and lovely items to hang on your walls. You might also create cards to send to your friends or just enjoy the pleasure of painting.

Setting up your easel is the start of an adventure in vision. You see so much more when you are trying to put your interpretation down on canvas. There are many classes, internet study groups, and books to help you get started. You need a few tools and an old shirt to protect your clothes. There is no reason why you can't just start having a go yourself in the privacy of your home, but watercolor painting can also be a group activity.

Imagine meeting a few like-minded people, setting up your easels in a spot where the view is stunning, and having an experienced artist to help you create your own vision to take home with you.

CROQUET

Croquet originated in Ireland and was exported to England in 1852 under the name "crookey," which means a hooked stick. However, croquet arrived in Australia as early as 1881 and is now seen as an ideal game for men and women well into their 80s. Since the population of Australia is aging, the game is booming.

It's also a great family game, with youngsters joining in on equal terms. (It's also a great way to meet people of the opposite sex, according to Pippa Middleton.) The game is not particularly energetic or competitive, but it is full of strategy and tactics for serious players and requires considerable skill. It can be referred to as "chess on grass."

The game is played with a mallet to hit the balls through a series of hoops or "wickets." Nowadays, the balls are made not from wood but a composite plastic and the types of plastic used affect the durability, weight, and bounce of the balls. Games usually last about 30 minutes.

Croquet can be an excuse for a party. When Sean "Puffy" Combs was accepted onto the Hollywood Walk of Fame, he held a $2 million croquet party. People in Tasmania also played croquet at Christmas picnics, although tennis did oust the popularity of croquet for a while.

There are club-level games and international world championships. The UK, Australia, New Zealand, and the US compete for the MacRobertson Shield every four years.

All you need is a lawn, wickets, some balls, and mallets, plus a few people to play with, and you are set to go. Croquet is gentle exercise, a lot of fun, and an excellent hobby for all ages.

LOCAL HISTORY

Between 65,000 and 50,000 years ago, people journeyed to Australia from Southeast Asia to make it their home. They traveled as far as Tasmania; they penetrated the northern forests and even eked out a living in the arid central deserts. And they left their marks as described in the rock art of the shelters.

The traditions these early Australians established are among the oldest in the world. They have their music, their artistic remnants, and especially their spiritual heritage.

And then along came the Europeans.

First were the Dutch, then the famous James Cook from England, who charted the east coast. The first fleet of British ships to arrive in Botany Bay came in 1788, and they started the first penal colony. More settlements were established, and Europeans penetrated far inland. The indigenous population was weakened by imported disease and by brutal conflicts with the settlers.

Gradually the prosperity of Australia increased, and modern Australia has welcomed over six million immigrants from every continent. As a result, trade is worldwide, and Australians have a wide range of museums and art galleries where people can begin to learn about their history and the history of this vast country.

The history of the Indigenous population is full of interest and a revival in the awareness of art, such as convict art and rock shelter paintings, which has stimulated both pride and belonging.

Local history can give you a feeling of belonging, too. Surprises may emerge from the local streets and villages, the local fields and woods, and the seas and rivers around you. There are often local history groups, meeting to explore your local places of interest. In addition, the internet and the local library often have a wealth of information just waiting for you to discover.

Local history might be allied to family history. The best is that you can do it even when it is pouring rain, and you don't want to venture outside.

SUMMARY

Australia is gigantic. The center of this enormous island is a hot desert, yet there are links to an ancient past. Rock art is deserving of respect, but you can make your own little link to the past by pebble painting. Another fascinating feature of Australia, especially Tasmania, is the lovely paintings that record the history of the early convict settlements; watercolor painting is one way to record your own history.

Indeed, local history can reveal some captivating and surprising facts about the place where you live. Local libraries often contain a wealth of information. And if, after all that "head work," you require a little gentle exercise with your friends or family, croquet is an ideal way to socialize without stress.

Australia has so much to offer, and I can only suggest a few ideas, but the links with the past, both ancient and more recent, make this a fascinating country. The chances are that you, too, live in an area where the past can speak to you.

    Rock art and pebble painting
    Watercolors
    Croquet
    Local history

LATVIA

The country of Latvia is a flattish plain filled with forests and the scent of pine trees. While there are some uplands to the east, grassy meadows and rolling hills make up most of the country. Yet, despite that plain description, Latvia has been voted the "most beautiful country in the world" several times.

Everywhere you go there are forests. They line the roads; they line the coast. There you find a rich harvest of lingonberries, bilberries, and mushrooms.

The Latvians do have a rather unusual sport – that of wife (or woman) carrying. These contests are thought to have originated in the 1800s when women were forcibly abducted. The Latvian style of carrying your wife is to have her hanging her head down your back with her legs over your shoulder, and you hang onto her lower legs and feet. They have special obstacle races, and the team with the fastest time wins.

But there are some more modern activities, so let's have a look at some of them.

MUSHROOM FORAGING

Latvians love mushrooms! Indeed, it is remarkable that there are any left in the forests after the autumn "shroomers" have been out foraging. But every year, many Latvians fill their fridges with the spoils from the woods – and it's free.

This hobby doesn't require a great deal of energy, so it is suitable for older people, who also bring their wisdom to the forest. It's healthy and takes you outside into the lovely countryside to fill the senses with pleasure and revitalize the brain cells.

Everywhere you look in the forests of Latvia, you can see people, heads down, straw hats on, carrying baskets filled with mushrooms. All you need is a knife and some knowledge of what you are collecting. Well, maybe more than a little...

The death cap, the deadliest of mushrooms, looks very similar to some edible mushrooms and is the most common source of mushroom poisoning. Death caps may have killed Emperor Claudius in 54 CE and Emperor Charles VI in 1740.

And even after the day exploring nature, there is the thrill of sorting your find, storing it, possibly even selling some of it, and the final triumph – mushrooms on toast for supper.

There are about 1,100 species of cap mushrooms, and you can eat three hundred of them, but most harvesters stick to the thirty or so types that they are familiar with. You may come across the golden-orange chanterelle, and you can be extra safe here since worms do not like them.

Then there are the boletus, which has no gills but instead has tubes for the spores beneath. They are excellent for drying and strong in taste. And there are so many more.

Here is a recipe for Latvian mushroom sauce:

Wild mushrooms, onion, ham (if you like ham), all chopped and fried together.

Then add sweet or sour cream with salt and pepper to taste. What could be simpler?

While mushrooming is a great hobby, it's best to start off in a group with someone who knows the types of mushrooms that are safe to eat. Many places have autumn mushroom foraging expeditions, and afterward, sorting your catch out in company is a great way to make friends. Of course, you also need a good reference book.

WEAVING

Archeology has unearthed some of the ancient crafts in Latvia, and weaving was of prime importance.

Around 2000 BCE, linen and wool were available in the early stone age, and different weaving techniques were developed, although we do not have traces of such early garments.

However, we do have bronze age fragments of clothing from the second to fourth century CE. Most of these are made from fleece, with traces of blue and red dyes still just discernible. These colors are often referred to in the Latvian folk songs or 'dainas.' You might also see yellow and dark brown. Because linen and hemp do not preserve well, they are most often found when combined with wool. And that meant some kind of weaving took place, with frames for the purpose, as long ago as Neolithic times.

Latvians also developed weaving that gave a tight and, therefore, warm fabric – needed in the cold dark winters. Latvian tribes were wearing plain fabrics of the "two-shaft" method by 100 CE, and by the 12th century, the "three-shaft" method, whereby diagonal lines were created, was also popular.

About this time, the horizontal weaving frame was introduced. Later on, weavers from Holland, France, and Germany introduced their techniques to the Latvians, who added them to their own traditional weaving techniques.

The Kurzeme cloths produced in the 16th and 17th centuries were highly regarded and a valuable export as well as a local commodity. Then, national costume and household textiles became increasingly crucial to Latvians, and their decorative weaving patterns are much admired.

Organized courses in weaving combine tradition and experience to enable others to produce fine artwork, and the State Museum preserves this Latvian heritage for us to enjoy.

Homemade textiles have value and uniqueness all of their own, and weaving as a hobby is entirely possible. The finished product makes lovely gifts, they can be sold, and most of all, they give you the pleasure of designing your own unique textiles.

You may be lucky enough to find local courses available, but in any case, there are many kits you can buy, videos you can watch and books you can read.

If you decide to try weaving, you will need some basic equipment:

1. A loom. This is the frame and comes in many sizes.
2. Shuttles.
3. A comb.
4. Tapestry needle.
5. Pair of scissors.
6. The thread.

To start off, you can use a piece of solid cardboard instead of buying a loom, but you will need a lot of yarn, so it is a great way to use up all those balls of wool you have never got around to knitting up.

Is weaving hard? It's as hard as you make it. The techniques are simple enough, but the patterns you make can be quite exciting and interesting.

DAINAS

These little four-liner folk songs allow us a glimpse into the past. There are over 1.2 million Dainas, and some were created over a thousand years ago. They recount daily life, celebrations, work, and reflections on people's lives.

Some Dainas celebrate Latvians' ancient pre-Christian gods and goddesses; others are about the mundane, everyday happenings, such as births where the mother figure appears to determine the child's fate. Like many religions, there is a sun goddess and a moon god.

Some Dainas mock; others are erotic. Some prepare a person for death, and of course, there are demons (who could be both good and bad) and an afterlife. In sum, they are a rich source of philosophy and beliefs.

Although the more usual heroic personages are absent, they allow us some insight into their legends and myths. Many Dainas have been translated into English.

I doubt that you can put so many rich thoughts into a four-liner, but it would be a unique way of keeping a diary and would undoubtedly make you think before you write. How could you put a day's experience into such a small poem, and does your Daina have a tune?

Writing your own Dainas could be a thought-provoking hobby and something to leave for posterity if you so wished.

POTTERY

We can date Latvian pottery to the Neolithic period; it is one of the country's most ancient forms of art.

Latvian pottery typically does not have patterns painted on but instead is a rich tapestry of solid colors and gradients. Traditionally, earth colors like brown and green were used, but modern artists have started inserting brighter colors onto their palettes. You can find mottled glazes and unusual shapes in the items produced nowadays.

Latgalian pottery

The region of Latgale is famous for its Latgalian pottery. Historically, Latgale produced pots for cooking, pots for storing sour cream, pots for fruit, and pots for honey, as well as pots for oil storage, pots for milk, and pots with handles for transporting – perhaps food for the workers in the fields?

Now the area produces modern ceramics, as well as some based on the ancient black ceramics from archeological discoveries, with little color.

Latgale pottery also includes figurines, candlesticks, decorative plates, and other contemporary items.

Pottery can be a fascinating hobby, but it does require some expenditure. The most expensive item is the kiln. Although there are ways of using your oven, especially if you are doing this with children, the results are often brittle and disappointing. But if you are prepared to invest in time for a course, and a little money for essential equipment, then you will be able to produce beautiful pots to adorn your home. Alternatively, you may be able to find a pottery studio that lets you take classes and use their kiln.

It's wise to learn from a professional potter before splashing out on your own. They can help you decide on the type of pottery you would like to make and guide you as to the equipment you will need, plus you might have a go at using the wheel!

SUMMARY

Latvia is a beautiful country of forests and more forests. No wonder foraging for mushrooms is so popular. This is an autumn activity you might enjoy – just be sure you know what you are collecting before eating it. Many places have mushroom foraging walks where you can discuss your findings with an expert.

Weaving is an ancient art, and if you want to try your hand, there are many kits available.

Pottery is another practical, ancient art. It makes a nice hobby but is best started by enrolling in a course and be guided by an experienced potter, as it is rather expensive to purchase your own materials and kiln. The feeling of the clay can be very therapeutic.

You might want to try your hand at writing a Daina. It could be another way to keep a journal.

    Mushroom foraging
    Weaving
    Daina writing
    Pottery

JAPAN

Are you interested in living a longer and healthier life? Why do you want to get up in the mornings? What pulls you out of bed each day?

What can we learn from Japan, home of the longest-living people, and where seniors enjoy an active, healthy life with purpose.

We will take our lessons from some key Japanese words: Ikigai, Hanami, Kintsugi, Kyudo, Origami, Haiku, and Onsen, which describe some very captivating hobbies.

IKIGAI

Ikigai is the reason why you get up in the morning. It's made of two words – "iki," meaning "life," and "gai," representing value. The word is not so much about the meaning of life as the joy in living. And since many of the oldest people in the world are Japanese, there must be some value in this concept.

Ikigai is different for different people. Work might be your ikigai (32% of Japanese consider this their ikigai), but it can equally well be related to family, to a love of travel, or to hobbies. Ikigai may appear to change as the person's life circumstances change, but when you look deeper, the change is superficial. The intrinsic values that drive the way a person experiences life remain the same: deep-seated and often unnoticed, they form the very core of a person's life.

So, let us look at some of the ways this attention to detail is a part of Japanese culture.

HANAMI

Hanami is the term used for the appreciation of cherry blossom trees. People take the time to sit and admire them and have parties to celebrate the brief span of time when the cherry blossom trees are in flower – between mid-March and early May.

Families and friends may gather to eat and drink under the blossom as the petals gently drift down upon them. Or someone may sit alone, lost in quiet contemplation.

Have you ever reached up to feel the super softness of the cherry blossom petals?

These cherry trees are known as Sakura, and they differ from ordinary cherry trees in that they are bountiful in pink and white blossom but do not produce fruit. Each tree is only in flower for a week or two, which reminds us of the transience of life and how precious every moment is.

This is an ancient tradition, going back hundreds of ears to the Naro period (710 – 794). Originally inspired by the Chinese, the "ume" plant was then admired, whose blooms lasted nearly two months. And then, the Japanese noticed the beauty of the Sakura, and this became their focus of appreciation. Poetry, literature, and philosophy have all been inspired by the blossom, both in Japan and China.

The bounty doesn't end in spring, for in autumn, people return to admire the turning of the leaves from green to red and gold. You might feel inspired by this to create a little space in a crowded life to imbibe the essence of nature. What beauty is around the corner in your neighborhood?

KINTSUGI

Kintsugi is a traditional Japanese craft where a broken vessel is repaired using a gold bonded resin. This fills the cracks and results in an even more beautiful item.

According to legend, this all started when a Japanese shogun sent a broken bowl to China to be repaired. The result was ugly – metal staples had been inserted to hold the pot together.

The local craftsmen thought they could make a better repair, and they experimented with new ways to mend the broken ceramic. Eventually, they discovered the gold bonded resin, and the process came to be known as kintsugi.

So impressed were the people with this new method of repair that they are said to have deliberately broken their pots to make them even more handsome when repaired with the gold-based resin.

If you look deeper into kintsugi, for the Japanese, it is a reminder that we are not perfect, to see beauty in that which is incomplete. In the process of healing ourselves, say after a break-up or a loss of some sort, we can learn to accept and celebrate our scars and imperfections and realize that we may have become even more unique and special with a newfound resilience. If you look closely at the art of kintsugi, the gold bond emphasizes the flaws within.

If you get the chance to visit Japan, be sure to search out this beautiful art form that may inspire you to start a creative project at home.

KYUDO

Japanese archery, or Kyudo, is a highly skilled sport, requiring dedication, practice, and more practice. Attention to detail and complete focus are needed to succeed, but all ages can participate.

The archers wear a specific costume: a kimono, very wide loose pants, and on their feet, tabo – socks with a thick sole and a separate part for the big toe.

The bows used are the longest in the world – up to 6 feet (2 meters) long – and they send arrows speeding out at 120 miles per hour (190 km per hour.)

Why are the bows so long? It's to stop them from breaking, as the longer the bow, the less force needed to draw it. But, given this length, the pull at the halfway mark of the bowstring is weak. So the archer does not pull at the halfway mark; they pull at a point one-third of the way up from the bottom. This is a sweet spot: the pull is strong, but the vibrations are weak, so a combination of greater power and accuracy can be achieved.

The accuracy can be astonishing. It's not just the physical power of the pull or the direction of the aim: it's a psychological preparation and mental state of mind that speeds the arrow to the target. The master Takeo Ishikawa demonstrated this spiritual training; he sent an arrow flying to the center of a distant target – in the dark!

The arrows preferred for use in competitions are the traditional bamboo arrows, made with great care. Carbon fiber arrows are often used in practice, but they are not as accurate as the traditional bamboo ones.

Every January, there is a long shot archery festival, and now Kyudo is practiced by thousands of people worldwide. A fascinating hobby, not for everyone but indeed a hobby to ponder.

ORIGAMI

Origami is a peaceful occupation possibly invented by the Japanese about 1000 years ago, but most likely had its roots in China. Now origami is a worldwide hobby, with special papers and many books of instructions. From paper airplanes sent by mischievous boys in the classroom to an activity for residents in a senior facility, origami can find a home anywhere.

Papermaking was invented in China around 105 CE and imported to Japan by Buddhist monks. By 610 CE, the Japanese were improving the quality of their paper, and it became suitable for origami, although it may not have been used as such back then. However, in 1680, a short poem by Ihara Saikaku mentions butterfly origami, revealing that the hobby of origami was well known. This is the short poem:

Rosei-ga yume-no cho-wa orisue.
(The butterfly in Rosie's dream would be origami.)

Originally, the art of folding probably applied to other materials – cloth, leather, even leaves. We still fold napkins in extravagant ways, and we may find our towels folded to resemble flowers or swans in upmarket hotels or onboard luxury liners, often just for the fun of it!

The value of origami also extends into teaching: it helps children to develop listening skills, take turns and cooperate, observe, follow directions, and to be patient.

Origami promotes confidence when the task is completed, helps to improve one's memory, and aids concentration. People with arthritis have found it helpful to release some of the tension from stiff fingers and strengthen the fine muscles in their hands.

Origami is calming and can be enjoyed alone or in groups, and is justifiably popular throughout the world. With a good book of instruction, Origami can be enjoyed in any part of the world. All you need is the required paper which you can always order online.

THE HAIKU

A haiku is a short, formal poem originating from Japan. It has a strict pattern and concentrates the mind wonderfully to ease out the essence of what you are trying to convey.

The traditional form has three phrases with a five-seven-five syllable pattern. The Japanese tend to write it on one line, whereas we use three lines in the West, as it's easier to read. The lines do not rhyme.

So the first line has five syllables, the second line seven, and the last line just five syllables again. Here is an example:

The Old Pond by Matsuo Basho
An old silent pond
A frog jumps into the pond—
Splash! Silence again.

And another haiku:

A World of Dew by Kobayashi Issa
A world of dew,
And within every dewdrop

A world of struggle.

How can one say so much with so few words? For all you word-lovers, writing a haiku could make an excellent hobby. I've started my collection of personally written haikus. But I'm not ready to share them with the world just yet.

ONSEN

You may be wondering how the Japanese relax. Japan is part of the Pacific Ring of Fire, where tectonic plates meet and volcanoes are born. So naturally, there are a great many hot springs. They are mentioned in Japan's oldest history book, written around 700 AD.

Many kinds of hot springs exist, from open-air examples to baths inside small hotels and hostels. The minerals in the water vary too, including calcium, sodium bicarbonate, sulfur, and iron. These minerals are absorbed through the skin while you lie back and relax, conferring many benefits to your health.

But entering Japan's hot baths is not the same as in most other countries. There is a strong and strict etiquette to be followed. This ensures your visit is pleasant and that every visitor can also have an enjoyable experience.

Originally men and women bathed naked together, but that is no longer always the case. Segregation of the sexes and swimming costumes or the special bathing "yakata" – a kind of kimono – is common, especially in tourist areas.

Cleanliness is still very much a part of the culture. You wash before entering the water. It is socially unacceptable to go in dirty or to drink alcohol there. But they make this easy by supplying well-stocked bathing stations where there is everything you need to get yourself spotless: soap, shampoo, taps, and buckets to ensure you wash off every trace of soap.

Then you can enjoy a relaxing hot soak in temperatures around 40°C. Even if the place is big, swimming is not encouraged.

Onsen has a dual purpose: cleanliness and relaxation.

You may not have an onsen close to you, but what other ways could you induce relaxation closer to home? I have seen beautiful spas in many places where one can go for a soak and relaxation. Many individuals have purchased a hot tub or infrared sauna to put in their homes for regular sessions to relax the body and mind. You may not consider this exactly a hobby, but one could participate in some form of relaxation on a regular basis.

SUMMARY

Japan melds the inner spirit and the outer life into a harmonious whole, and the life expectancy of the Japanese is longer than most.

Ikigai is a state of mind; it's your core value – why you get up in the morning. Finding yours can give you inner strength and serenity.

The Hanami, or cherry blossom, gives time for reflection in a natural setting to further this sense of calmness.

Kintsugi will restore your broken ceramics and make them even more beautiful.

Kyudo, Japanese archery, combines careful knowledge of the physical properties of the bow and the arrow – another example of taking note of the detail. Archery is a fine hobby for some of us.

Origami is practiced worldwide – this can be a great teaching aid in patience and persistence as well as a nice little hobby for anyone.

Onsen is a calming way to relax using the hot springs, but you might have to make do with a warm bath, which is still relaxing. However, if there are hot springs near you, they are worth a visit.

When the evening comes, and you need a rest, why not try your hand at writing a haiku? It's not easy to put so few words together in a meaningful way. You might have to dig deep into your mind to construct a little masterpiece.

>
> Ikigai – a state of mind
> Hanami – appreciation
> Kintsugi – beauty in imperfection
> Kyudo – Japanese archery
> Origami – paper folding
> Haiku – short poems
> Onsen – hot spring bathing

THE UNIVERSAL HOBBY

Our final hobby is to do nothing – nothing at all. But not in the passive, negative way our friend Harry (whom you met in the introduction) did nothing. There is a far better and different way to free your mind completely.

When you master this, you will find that your mind is more open to challenges, more confident in its ability to master them, and freer to engage in new activities.

It's like a painting. Generally speaking, one prefers to paint on a clean canvas, not cluttered with past efforts and mistakes. Your brain is the same. So, this is how you do it:

This is best done in a darkened room with you sitting comfortably and relaxed.

- Drop your shoulders to release tension and breath evenly and steadily.
- Now, light a candle. This should be unscented since you do not want to stimulate any of your senses.
- Gaze at the candle.
- Immerse your thoughts in the flame. Watch it as it flickers. Admire its many colors.
- Then – and this is the crux – if ANY thought comes into your mind, place it gently in a bubble and let it waft away. To start with, you may have to give it a gentle blow, but soon you will find you can just let the bubbles disappear on their own.

This can be incredibly hard to do.

At first, you might only be able to clear your mind for a moment, but with practice, you might extend the time to several seconds.

Some people practice candle gazing in many parts of the world. Some get so good at it that they can dispense with the candle and simply "candle gaze" without the candle. The brief moments of total control and a completely clear brain can reinvigorate them, resetting their inner self.

Why not try it and see how far you can get.

Candle gazing

FINAL THOUGHTS

You have traveled around the world, visiting new places and picking up new ideas along the way from people just like you.

While you might not be able to replicate all of these hobbies exactly, a few minor creative modifications are all it takes to turn even the most exotic activity into your new retirement pastime.

I hope that this book has been enlightening and given you ideas to follow and make your own. There is only this one life, and we all deserve to live it and enjoy it as much as we possibly can.

Don't be afraid to try something new. One of my favorite quotes is by Wayne W. Dyer and goes like this, "Go for it now. The future is promised to no one."

You might have ideas for some more unusual or interesting hobbies, and I would love to hear about them – and maybe include them in a future book. Please email me at: ravina@ravinachandra.com. I look forward to connecting with you.

People are inventive and exciting – I loved researching this book, and I hope you have enjoyed reading it.

INDEX

Accordion playing, Chapter 9, Austria
Ancient history, Chapter 6, Greece
Amulet collecting, Chapter 2, Thailand
Armchair caving, Chapter 15, Brazil
Art and sculpture appreciation, Chapter 11, Italy

Bird watching, Chapter 6, Greece
Beekeeping, Chapter 7, New Zealand
Board games, Chapter 7, New Zealand
Bobbin lace-making, Chapter 16, Portugal
Book clubs, Chapter 7, New Zealand
Boules, Chapter 4, France
Breakfast on the boulevard, Chapter 4, France

Calligraphy, Chapter 13, China
Camper van or RV exploration, Chapter 5, Canada
Candle gazing, Chapter 22, All or Any Country
Canning and preserving, Chapter 7, New Zealand
Canoeing, Chapter 16, Portugal

210 | INDEX

Carnival, Chapter 15, Brazil
Cheese bread making, Chapter 15, Brazil
Cheesemaking, Chapter 14, The Netherlands
Chess, Chapter 11, Italy
Choirs, Chapter 7, New Zealand
Collecting, *see Amulet collecting or Collecting plastic bags*
Collecting plastic bags, Chapter 10, Singapore
Cricket, Chapter 17, Fiji
Crochet clubs, Chapter 7, New Zealand
Croquet, Chapter 19, Australia
Cruising, *see River cruising*
Curling, Chapter 5, Canada
Cycling, Chapter 4, France

Daines writing, Chapter 20, Latvia
Day trips to the sea, Chapter 1, The United Kingdom
Drinking British style, Chapter 1, The United Kingdom
Drumming, Chapter 18, The Gambia

Eco-gardening, Chapter 7, New Zealand
Embroidery, Chapter 16, Portugal

Fandango and Fado, Chapter 16, Portugal
Fairy tale writing, Chapter 12, Denmark
Family trees, Chapter 13, China
Feng Shui, Chapter 13, China
Fine Dining, Chapter 1, The United Kingdom
Flower growing and arranging, Chapter 14, The Netherlands

Garage sales, Chapter 3, Belgium
Garden gnomes, Chapter 8, Germany
Gardening, *see Eco-gardening*

INDEX | 211

Genealogy, *see Family trees*
Geocaching, Chapter 8, Germany
Ghost hunting, Chapter 3, Belgium
Gnomes, *see Garden gnomes*
Go on an historical outing, Chapter 1, The United Kingdom

Haiku, Chapter 21, Japan
Hot Air Ballooning, Chapter 3, Belgium
Hanami, Chapter 21, Japan
Hand signals, Chapter 11, Italy

Ice skating, Chapter 14, The Netherlands
Ikigai, Chapter 21, Japan
Indoor waterfalls, Chapter 13, China

Jewelry from scrap and kits, Chapter 9, Austria
Jigsaw Puzzles, Chapter 3, Belgium
Journaling and blogging, Chapter 10, Singapore

Kayaking, Chapter 16, Portugal
Kintsugi, Chapter 21, Japan
Kyudo, Chapter 21, Japan

Lace-making, *see Bobbin lace-making*
Lavender bags or candles, Chapter 4, France
Lego, Chapter 12, Denmark
Local history, Chapter 19, Australia
Lovo underground cooking, Chapter 17, Fiji

Mini libraries, Chapter 5, Canada
Mosaics, Chapter 11, Italy
Mushroom foraging, Chapter 20, Latvia

Mythology, Chapter 6, Greece

Nature trails, Chapter 17, Fiji

Olive appreciation, Chapter 6, Greece
Onsen, Chapter 21, Japan
Opera, Chapter 11, Italy
Origami, Chapter 21, Japan

Paintball, Chapter 16, Portugal
Papermaking, Chapter 13, China
Patchwork, Chapter 3, Belgium
Pebble painting, *see Rock art and pebble painting*
Photography - *see Sightseeing and photography*
Pickleball, Chapter 5, Canada
Pottery, Chapter 20, Latvia
Preserving, *see Canning and preserving*

Random acts of kindness, Chapter 13, Denmark
River cruising, Chapter 8, Germany
Rock art and pebble painting, Chapter 19, Australia
Runes, Chapter 13, Denmark

Samba, Chapter 15, Brazil
Scuba diving, Chapter 2, Thailand
Sculptures, *see Art and sculpture appreciation*
Sightseeing and photography, Chapter 1, United Kingdom
Sign language, *see Hand signals*
Singing, *see Choirs*
Soap carving, Chapter 2, Thailand
Speakers' Club, Chapter 1, The United Kingdom
Swimming in the sea, Chapter 7, Greece

Tai chi, Chapter 13, China
Take an educational course, Chapter 1, The United Kingdom
Tatort, Chapter 8, Germany
Tavli, Chapter 6, Greece
Tea drinking, Chapter 1, The United Kingdom
Thai cookery, Chapter 2, Thailand
Theatre groups, Chapter 9, Austria
Toy voyagers, Chapter 8, Germany

U3A, Chapter 9, New Zealand
Underground cooking, *see Lovo underground cooking*

Virtual reality, Chapter 10, Singapore

Watercolors, Chapter 19, Australia
Weaving, Chapter 20, Latvia
Wine appreciation, Chapter 4, France
Wood carving, Chapter 18, The Gambia
Writing, *see Fairy tale writing or Daines writing*

Yodelling, Chapter 9, Austria
Yoga, Chapter 2, Thailand

REFERENCES

Australia

"Lost World of the Kimberley" by Ian Wilson

https://mail.google.com/mail/u/0/?pli=1#inbox/FMfcgzGkZkXNDrHppnwknFbDGnTQlgzm

https://learnantiques.com.au/historical-tasmanian-artists-part-2-four-australian-born-artists/

https://www.vanityfair.com/culture/2015/05/pippa-middleton-croquet-guide

Austria

https://blog.goodybeads.com/tutorial/diy-jewelry-with-swarovski-around-the-world-austria/

Belgium

https://archive.curbed.com/2014/1/2/10158982/frances-abandoned-chateau-miranda-is-a-ghost-hunters-paradise https://theculturetrip.com/europe/belgium/articles/belgiums-10-spookiest-spots/

Brazil

https://www.oliviascuisine.com/authentic-brazilian-cheese-bread/

China

https://fengshuinexus.com/feng-shui-rules/what-is-feng-shui/

https://luxurylaunches.com/travel/china-will-get-indoor-waterfall-almost-high-niagara-falls.php

https://www.familysearch.org/blog/en/chinese-family-tree-jiapu/

https://www.calligraphy-skills.com/italic-lettering.html

Denmark

https://www.legoland.dk/en/

https://www.lego.com/en-us/aboutus/news/2019/october/lego-campus-grand-opening/

Fiji

https://www.motherearthnews.com/real-food/how-to-build-your-own-earth-oven-zmaz78jazbur

France

https://www.chartreuse.fr/en/visites/chartreuse-cellars-in-voiron-special-english-guided-tour/

https://www.vinotrip.com/en/images lavender fields

Germany

https://www.geocaching.com/blog/2013/02/celebrating-two-million-geocaches-list-by-country/

https://www.postcrossing.com/blog/2014/05/15/toyvoyagers

Greece

https://learn.oliveoilschool.org/

https://www.mysteriousgreece.com/mood/activities/

https://www.ornithologiki.gr/en/

Italy

https://www.gonomad.com/1766-italian-hand-gestures-in-conversation

Latvia

https://en.wikipedia.org/wiki/Daina_(Latvia)

New Zealand

https://www.aucklandforkids.co.nz/toys-games/best-family-board-games/

https://www.rnz.co.nz/concert/programmes/musicalive/audio/2018713707/the-big-sing-2019-gala-concert-first-half

Portugal

http://EzineArticles.com/8965247

Singapore

https://www.capitalsenior.com/virtual-reality-allows-seniors-to-experience-a-whole-new-world-right-at-their-fingertips/

https://www.barfboutique.com/lasticos

https://mapletreemedia.com/famous-blog-in-singapore/

Thailand

https://mymodernmet.com/soap-carving-narong-thai/

https://www.wikihow.com/Make-a-Soap-Carving

http://woodcarvingillustrated.com/blog/2018/04/05/carving-a-soap-flower/

The Netherlands

https://cheesemaking.com/products/edam-cheese-making-recipe

https://www.kaasworkshops.nl/en/make-cheese-or-butter/

The UK

https://www.nationaltrust.org.uk/

https://www.english-heritage.org.uk/

https://www.heritagetrustnetwork.org.uk/about-us/areas/northern-ireland/

https://www.historicenvironment.scot/

https://cadw.gov.wales/

IMAGE CREDITS

Introduction

Active Senior photo courtesy of mgfoto, Pixabay.com, Pixabay License

Australia

1399 (Kangaroo) photo courtesy of Andrew Bertuleit, Pixabay.com, Pixabay License

Watercolor Map of Australia. Watercolour Illustration photo courtesy of undrey's images, Pixabay.com, Pixabay License

Austria

Accordion photo courtesy of tellmemoreooo, Pixabay.com, Pixabay License

Salzburg, Austria photo courtesy of sorincolac, Pixabay.com, Pixabay License

Volkstheater in Vienna Austria at Night photo courtesy of and.one, Pixabay.com, Pixabay License

Belgium

Hot Air Balloons courtesy of JMartinPhotography, Pixabay.com, Pixabay License

Patchwork photo courtesy of philipimage, Pixabay.com, Pixabay License

Brazil

Cave, Ubajara National Park, Brazil photo courtesy of tunart, Pixabay.com, Pixabay License

Favela houses in Brazil photo courtesy of Aliaksei Skreidzeleu, Pixabay.com, Pixabay License

Pao de Queijo photo courtesy of AndreaGoldschmidt, Pixabay.com, Pixabay License

Canada

Curling Woman photo courtesy of nojustice, Pixabay.com, Pixabay License

Free outdoor library photo courtesy of ImageGolf, Pixabay.com, Pixabay License

Park RV in Camp Site photo courtesy of anonymous, Pixabay.com, Pixabay License

China

Caligraphy practice photo courtesy of BVBeckman, Pixabay.com, Pixabay License

Chinese Calligraphy photo courtesy of SteveAllenPhoto, Pixabay.com, Pixabay License

Feng Shui balance photo courtesy of zeleno, Pixabay.com, Pixabay License

Rain vortex at Jewel Changi Airport, Changi, Singapore photo courtesy of William Chng, Pixabay.com, Pixabay License

Denmark

Nyhavn photo courtesy of SuppalakKlabdee, Pixabay.com, Pixabay License

Runic Stone photo courtesy of Plougmann, Pixabay.com, Pixabay License

Untitled lego photo courtesy of Efraimstochter, Pixabay.com, Pixabay License

Fiji

Fijian Food Lovo in Fiji Islands photo courtesy of chameleonseye, Pixabay.com, Pixabay License

Tropical beach photo courtesy of Nurture, Pixabay.com, Pixabay License

France

champagne photo courtesy of lea dubois, Pixabay.com, Pixabay License

vineyard and medieval church in Alsace, France photo courtesy of Milena Pigdanowicz-Fidera, Pixabay.com, Pixabay License

Woman riding on an adult tricycle photo courtesy of Creatas, Pixabay.com, Pixabay License

Gambia

Djembe players photo courtesy of peeterv, Pixabay.com, Pixabay License

Flag of Gambia photo courtesy of enigma_images, Pixabay.com, Pixabay License

Germany

BERLIN, GERMANY photo courtesy of Aliaksei Skreidzeleu, Pixabay.com, Pixabay License

Dramatic sunset over river photo courtesy of Britus, Pixabay.com, Pixabay License

Garden Gnome photo courtesy of anela, Pixabay.com, Pixabay License

Greece

Greece photo courtesy of oversnap, Pixabay.com, Pixabay License

Olive Grove Tree Greece photo courtesy of Kloegoo8, Pixabay.com, Pixabay License

Italy

Cinque Terre, Italy photo courtesy of Walkerssk, Pixabay.com, Pixabay License

Hand gestures photo courtesy of mycan, Pixabay.com, Pixabay License

Mosaics in Ravenna, Italy photo courtesy of Flavio Valenari, Pixabay.com, Pixabay License

Japan

IMAGE CREDITS | 223

Kintsugi Japanese antique ceramic bowl photo courtesy of Marco Montalti, Pixabay.com, Pixabay License

Origami photo courtesy of paolaroid, Pixabay.com, Pixabay License

Young woman looking at cherry blossoms at hanami party photo courtesy of Santosh-k, Pixabay.com, Pixabay License

Latvia

Colorful pottery photo courtesy of inguuna, Pixabay.com, Pixabay License

Exotic mushrooms photo courtesy of Langan, Pixabay.com, Pixabay License

Famous square in old Riga city, Latvia photo courtesy of gorsch13, Pixabay.com, Pixabay License

New Zealand

Beekeeper Controlling Beeyard photo courtesy of Kzenon, Pixabay.com, Pixabay License

Crochet baby booties photo courtesy of gojak, Pixabay.com, Pixabay License

Portugal

Beautiful fado singer performing with handsome Portuguese guitarist, Portugal photo courtesy of Jacek_Sopotnicki, Pixabay.com, Pixabay License

Bobbin lace manufacturing courtesy of Mercedes Rancano Otero, Pixabay.com, Pixabay License.

Traditional historic facade in Porto decorated with blue tiles, Portugal photo courtesy of Mirifada, Pixabay.com, Pixabay License

Singapore

Colorful knitting from recycle plastic bag photo courtesy of prapassong, Pixabay.com, Pixabay License

Panorama of marina bay sand, garden by the bay and Singapore flyer photo courtesy of Pasu Lo-utai, Pixabay.com, Pixabay License

Thailand

Antique Thai Buddha amulets in an amulet market, Thailand photo courtesy of enviromantic, Pixabay.com, Pixabay License

Soap Carving Flower photo courtesy of Praiwun, Pixabay.com, Pixabay License

The Netherlands

traditional cheesemaking photo courtesy of nullplus, Pixabay.com, Pixabay License

Traditional dutch windmills and houses photo courtesy of Olena_Z, Pixabay.com, Pixabay License

United Kingdom

British Tea photo courtesy of Upyanose, Pixabay.com, Pixabay License

Untitled (Castle) photo courtesy of Graham_H, Pixabay.com, Pixabay Licensething

Universal Hobby

Candle Lit in Black Background photo courtesy of Jordi C, Pixabay.com, Pixabay License

101 MORE WAYS TO ENJOY RETIREMENT

INTRODUCTION

Retirement – at last.

The days are long and full of promise. But how do you fill them? How do you spend your long-awaited freedom?

Retiring opens the door to a bewildering range of activities you never had time for before. This book looks at ways people enjoy their hobbies in 21 countries around the world. You will find many hobbies you are familiar with and some that are new to you. Some you will pass by quickly, but others you might find intriguing.

When Fran retired from a busy life managing a retail company, she decided to put her feet up, rest, relax – and do absolutely nothing.

This lasted for a whole ten days!

She was bored and lonely and didn't think life had anything left to offer her. But, as John Kennedy famously said in his inaugural speech on becoming president of the United States – "Think not what your country can do for you – think what you can do for your country."

Fran remembered these words as she watched yet another old TV series, which was a wake-up call. That night she felt excited, and her brain felt like it was going round and round in circles. Sleep just wouldn't come.

She knew she had to get some order into her life and realized it was down to her to go out and join in the social life around her. It was down to her to find interesting hobbies that challenged her. She knew she had an excellent opportunity to learn new skills, make new friends, and live each day fully and completely.

Keeping your interest in our wonderful world alive, is the best way to stay fit physically, but also mentally. People who socialize, take some form of exercise and stimulate their brains, by learning new things, are the ones who are happy in their later years.

Cooking is becoming increasingly popular, and you will find some delicious recipes to try out, share, and delight your friends and family. There are many other ways to use your creative skills: some you may already do, some you may have tried as a child, and some will be unexpected.

While you probably won't be advised to participate in combative sports like wrestling and boxing, for example, there are plenty of physical activities to keep you supple and fit. And you can always watch a football match and cheer your team on.

Age brings wisdom and a wealth of knowledge to our brains. It is a time when we can catch up on everything we never had time for. As you read this book, you will find the days are filled with excitement, and now you have time to appreciate and enjoy it.

My entire career has been in healthcare, and much of my time has been spent with older clients, who are often inspiring, unique, and always interesting. Engaging with them has stimulated my own life in so many ways.

I am hoping this book will help to enrich your life, even a very tiny bit. So, stay curious, stay adventurous, and dive in.

One more thing to mention before you delve into the pages of this book, as I know some of you are wondering why your country is missing.

For every chapter of this book, thorough research and interviews took place to ensure proper representation of hobbies and countries. First, check if your country was featured in my first hobbies book. If not, and you would like your country or hobby featured in an upcoming book, I would love to hear from you. A special shout-out to my American friends. What a vast and diverse country you have. Coming shortly is your very own, special edition of 101 Hobbies from Across the U.S.A.

Please get in touch with me with your ideas at:
ravina@ravinachandra.com

INDIA

The people of India (Indians) seem able to absorb cultures from all over the world. Like much of the world, modern hobbies include reading, social media, streaming television, and playing video games. Indians also enjoy the hobby of design creation, such as graphic design, excelling at this on a professional level too.

While reading might seem old-fashioned, the younger generation enjoys reading fiction – favoring fantasy, romance, and thrillers. Older people prefer non-fiction, including self-help, health, and business.

Indian residents were surveyed regarding what drives them and their passions. It was discovered that Indians take their leisure time seriously, with twenty-percent spending at least an hour a day on hobbies. In addition, three-quarters of the population spend a quarter of their salary on hobbies—a good life-work balance.

But there are some things that the Indian population are particularly good at. They also use their hobbies to make friends, and we know that good social interaction is excellent for our health. The hobbies I have chosen to represent India are a nice mixture of physically stimulating and mentally relaxing.

KITE FLYING

Uttarayan – the International Kite Festival, is primarily a Hindu festival that celebrates the day the sun transits into the Northern hemisphere and into the sign of Capricorn. This is the day known as Makar Sankranti – on the 14th of January or the 15th, depending on if it's a leap year. In the state of Gujarat and some other states in India, this is a two-day public holiday. It is one of the biggest festivals in India.

Makar Sankranti is when the gods awaken from their deep winter sleep.

The Rigged is an ancient Indian collection of Vedic Sanskrit hymns and mentions the festival 5,000 years ago. The Rigveda derives from the words for praise and knowledge and is one of four sacred Hindu texts known as the 'Vedas,' among the oldest surviving texts in any Indo-European language.

The ancient kings and Nawabs enjoyed the sport of kite flying, but now anyone can fly their kite – and people come from all over the world to revel in the entertainment.

People start preparing many weeks in advance. Apart from the kites, there are fine clothes and costumes to make and festive foods to prepare. It's an exciting time for the young and the old.

Throughout the kite flying week, the markets are full of colorful kites and all the accessories you could possibly want to enjoy this spectacle. In Gujarat, the town of Ahmedabad has one of the largest markets, and at the nearby riverfront, you might find up to 500,000 people, many lying down to watch the kites filling the skies overhead.

Kites come in various shapes and sizes, often influenced by their country of origin. For example, from Italy comes sculptured kites, from Japan comes fighting kites, and from China the spectacular dragon kites.

People make kites from many different materials – plastic, leaves, nylon, metal, wood, and an assortment of scrap materials. But the true Uttarayan kites are made from bamboo and lightweight paper. Most are rhomboid in shape, with a central spine and one bow. The kites are often brightly painted; a tiger may have stripes, and a dragon fiery breath.

You do not want to get in the way of the lines, either. They are commonly covered with glue and ground glass. After drying, they are rolled up and attached to the back of the kite and are called 'firkees' – razor-sharp. These 'patangs,' or fighter kites, are used to cut down the opponents' kites. Kite battles can be a cutthroat business!

If you want to make your own kite, they are not too hard to make – and you can decorate it in any way pleasing to you. Children or grandchildren may be keen to help. And flying can be exhilarating, out in the wind watching your creation sing up into the skies.

You can also buy readymade kits if you don't want to make them from scratch. Kite flying can be a friendly hobby – and once you have successfully flown your kite, you will want to do it again and again.

INDIAN CURRY MAKING

Curry is one of the most popular foods worldwide – but nothing can beat a good Indian curry.

India is a big country, so it is not surprising that there are an almost infinite number of local variations and seasonal varieties of curry. Everywhere you go in India, you can find exciting and nutritious curries. And of the eighty different spices worldwide – fifty are grown in India – they have hundreds of years of experience in their use.

Simple foods like potatoes can be turned into tasty and exotic dishes with the skillful use of herbs and spices.

Here is a list of ingredients for a spicy potato curry that runs something like this:

Potatoes
Onion
Tomatoes
Chili powder
Cumin seeds
Sprig of curry leaves
Ginger
Garlic
Salt
Turmeric
Coriander
Garam masala
Red chili powder

Optional:
Coconut milk
Mustard seeds
Bay leaf

Herbs and spices can make a dish taste delicious – many herbs and spices are also credited with medicinal properties. So, let us look at some of the most commonly used ingredients in Indian curry. Small changes in spices can create original and very different-tasting curries.

Apart from onions, cilantro, tomatoes, vegetable oils, and ginger, the common spices used are curry powder, turmeric, cayenne pepper, cloves, cardamom, fenugreek, and cumin.

What properties are credited to some of these spices?

Turmeric

Turmeric has a reputation as an anti-inflammatory, and we are beginning to recognize just how important this property is for our health and longevity. Turmeric treats arthritis and other inflammatory diseases and improves our immune system.

Cumin

Cumin is claimed to relieve toothaches and prevent certain diseases because of its antioxidant properties.

Fenugreek

Fenugreek is known to lower blood sugar levels in people with diabetes and help preserve food.

Coriander

Rich in immune-boosting antioxidants, coriander is good for coughs, allergies, and skin rashes. It also helps thicken gravy – and the fresh leaves make a delightful garnish.

Cloves

Cloves have been used for many years for their pain-relieving benefits to help tooth pain. In addition, some use cloves to ease digestive problems by brewing tea with cloves and ginger.

Cardamon

Cardamon may lower blood pressure due to its diuretic effect, promoting urination and removing water that builds up in your body. Using cardamon to treat bad breath and improve oral health has been an ancient remedy for years.

Cooking a curry can be mentally stimulating, not too tricky, and very rewarding. In addition, it is a great way to entertain guests, making it a wonderful hobby your friends will be pleased about.

MANDALA DRAWING

People from many countries have created mandalas. Often this is in the religious context but sometimes simply for the pleasure of creating a beautiful and ordered design. You can find them in Australian aborigines' cultures, Aztec civilizations, and Catholic Christianity.

The most common religions in the world are Christianity, Islam, and thirdly Hinduism, and about 80% of the Indian population are Hindus. But India is home to many other religions, including Islam, Christianity, Buddhism, Sikhs, and Jains.

Hinduism might be the oldest major religion globally and can be traced back 5,000 years or more – and mandalas are closely associated with Hindu and Buddhist meditations and art.

Mandalas serve as a guided pathway to enlightenment. They represent the universe and act as an aid to meditation, self-awareness, and finding one's way in the grand scheme of life.

The traditional mandala is circular in shape, symmetrical, and colored. Sometimes the circle is placed with a square with four T-shaped gates. It represents purity and enlightenment. Or it might represent the entire universe, with a sacred mountain in the center and the continents around it.

Mandalas may be used for teaching, healing, or as a guide to inner consciousness. They can help focus one's attention, clear distracting thoughts from the mind, and act as a map representing the gods in some religions. One works through the mandala from the outer edges to the central core.

The great thing about mandalas is that you can produce your own and give it an inner meaning right for you. Creating your mandala is also very relaxing, and many adult coloring books feature mandalas.

Mandalas can be drawn on paper or silk or made into wall hangings or rugs – even patchwork creations for quilts or throws. Whatever your skills are, a mandala can be a relaxing and instructive skill.

DESIGN AND MOOD BOARD CREATION

Indians love color and design, so it's no surprise that illustration and design are increasingly popular hobbies. Many of the best professional designers are Indians.

There are so many applications for your designs. For example, you may use it to make a book cover, cover cardboard boxes to make stylish storage containers, infographics on the internet, or perhaps design your clothing.

The idea behind graphic design is to make a visual representation of your thoughts. It can increase clarity in your mind, help you see the way through problems, and be an excellent way to communicate your ideas.

Fortunately, many online courses help you with your digital design start-up. If you do not want to use computers, you can still make a mood board with pictures, colors, and a little writing in different styles. Making a collage of your ideas can look attractive and help you sort out your mind.

Learning to make online digital designs takes effort and research – but the results can be remarkable. And one of the best things is that you can share your results with people on the other side of the world if you wish.

Mood Boards

A mood board is one way to put your ideas together visually, perhaps before creating your final design or simply as an attractive way to organize your thoughts.

It is easy to change the mood board as your ideas align with your new aspirations. Your mood board is a very personal thing – they can come in many guises – different shapes – different color co-ordinations – different styles.

Some things of note might be images like stock photos, personal memoirs, or drawings. Colors can help coordinate your theme, arrows can lead you from one part to another, and words can be in color, attractive fonts, and large enough to have an impact. Textures can be used for good effect, on-screen or in materials if your collage is physical.

But if you need help with this, you can find templates on the internet. For example, photoshop and Canva are well worth exploring. Instagram and Pinterest are just two sites where you might find a few ideas. Mood boards are fun to make, and creating your designs can be addictive.

SUMMARY

India is a vast continent with a huge variety of natural scenery, the second largest population globally, and many different outlooks on life. Yet they seem able to assimilate other cultures and adapt them to suit themselves.

Kite Flying
Curry Making
Mandela Drawing
Design and Mood Board Creation

SWEDEN

Sweden is the largest country in Northern Europe. It has massive forests, high mountains, and a long coastline with thousands of islands. Did you know that the capital city, Stockholm, is built on 14 islands and has over 50 bridges!

Sweden has long dark days in winter, encouraging Swedes to find indoor hobbies – so reading, playing games with family and friends, or putting around on the internet are popular hobbies.

Moderation in all things is a way of life in Sweden, which is reflected in their interior decorating. They have a worldwide reputation for clean lines and fuss-free furniture and homes. Crafts, music, and cooking are hobbies enjoyed by Sweden's people. I have picked out some hobbies that identify with their philosophy of life and their thoughtfulness for other people. So, let's have a look.

LAGOM

Lagom means 'just the right amount,' 'in balance,' 'suitable,' and so on...

The earliest examples are to be found in 17th-century texts. The word comes from 'lag' for 'law' or 'according to custom.' It has been suggested that the word 'lagom' is a contraction of 'laget om,' which means 'around the team' and is said to relate to how much mead one should drink from the Viking horn as it was passed around the hall so that all would be able to drink a fair share. A nice idea but probably not entirely true.

But as mentioned, the idea of moderation is an integral part of Swedish culture. Enough is as good as a feast. Greed and the accumulation of things you do not need are alien to most Swedes. Why have ten toothbrushes when you only use one at a time?

Other countries may have similar ideas with slightly different emphases. For example, just right, comfortable, or fine is another way of expressing how things seem and how you feel. Some countries with specific words for this idea of moderation include Norway, Finland, Albania, and Thailand. Even the ancient Greeks had a phrase meaning 'moderation is best.'

Maybe you are already a 'lagom' sort of person? If not, would taking on this concept be a good hobby for you? For example, decluttering your home environment over a period of time or aiming for a more minimalist attitude and existence might give you lagom.

There are various online programs to help with this way of life. It does tie into the Swedish character of 'enough is enough' and makes for a streamlined quality of life.

COFFEE CULTURE IN SWEDEN

'Fika' is a Swedish form of taking a coffee break, and always with a pastry or other snack. What better way to relax with your family and friends? It's not just a coffee with a to-go cup; it's a time to slow down and gather with friends or a moment on your own to reflect on your day.

In 2017, the Telegraph claimed that Swedes consumed more coffee than most other nations. The estimate was 8.2 kg per person per year. Since the early 1800s, coffee drinking has been part of the way of life for Swedes, and there is no sign of slowing down.

Any time of day will do; you do not need an excuse to drink coffee. But 11 a.m. is perhaps the favorite time to settle down with a cinnamon or cardamon bun and a cup of coffee. Many Swedes take a second Fika break later in the afternoon, around 3 p.m., especially if they work in an office environment.

So entrenched is the coffee culture that local bakeries have started opening up the front of their shops to form small cafes with fresh buns. This ritual certainly propels you to pause your busy day.

LÖRDAGSGODIS

Too much of a good thing palls, so a treat on Saturdays is something children can look forward to and enjoy. Adults with a sweet tooth can also look forward to an enjoyable part of their weekly routine.

'Lördagsgodis' means 'Saturday sweets or candy.' Since the 1950s, this has become a part of Swedish culture. They say that a little of what you like is good for you. And this applies to small quantities of sweets.

Sweets, as you know, contain sugar, are not great for your teeth, and incline people to obesity. As the country became wealthier, people had more to spend on treats. To limit increasing rates of tooth decay, the Swedish medical authorities recommended limiting sweets to once a week.

Swedish sweets generally do not contain trans fats, high-fructose corn syrup, or gluten, making them less harmful than candy that does include these ingredients.

One of the favorite Swedish treats is called Skumkantareller – which translates as Foam Mushrooms. They are shaped like mushrooms, are soft and chewy, and taste nothing like mushrooms.

Apart from the health benefits of limiting sweets, this Lördagsgodis teaches children (and adults!) to wait, plan ahead, and instill a little self-discipline. Maybe you have something a little 'naughty' you enjoy eating? Perhaps you would enjoy it even more if you limited it to just one day a week?

You could turn your hobby of making bread or pastries, for example, into a memorable event once a week or once a month.

SWEDISH SAUNA

Saunas in Sweden are often used as a great way to relax, even though Finland is where saunas are most used. There are a huge number of saunas in Sweden – often known as 'bastu.' Many are found in leisure centers, spas, and swimming pools.

Spas are very popular, and the tradition of a hot sauna followed by an icy dip, and maybe a wonderful Swedish massage could untie any knots in your muscles and make you feel on top of the world.

In the fifth century, saunas were found in shallow caves on the mountainsides. There you would find a hot stove with heated stones. As the water was poured into the rocks, steam rose, and the humidity increased – and so did the feeling of heat.

Then wooden buildings with iron stoves came into being. Mothers often gave birth in one of these saunas because they were immaculate, and post-natal infection was unlikely to occur. In the 18th century, saunas were considered hotbeds of immoral behaviors and outlawed. It was thought that they also encouraged the spread of syphilis.

The etiquette is simple, you enter naked but wrapped in a towel. In fact, the towel is essential to sit on. You must shower beforehand, and food and drink are not usually allowed in the sauna. It's just a matter of good manners. Sometimes the sexes are segregated but not generally, as nudity is generally well accepted by the Swedes.

Today, saunas are not only an excellent way to relax but are also known for their health benefits, including releasing toxins from your body, soothing aching muscles, and reducing inflammation.

For many tourists, a Swedish sauna is on their bucket list. But you could always make a habit of sauna use by purchasing one for your home or checking whether there are any in your local area. If buying a sauna is too much for you, another option is an infrared sauna blanket which is inexpensive and easy to use. Please do your sauna research, though, as there are many different makes and models, so find out what is best for you.

DÖSTÄDNING

'Dö' is death in Swedish, and 'städning' means standing or cleaning. You can also call it 'death cleaning.'

Times change. All those things you thought your grandchildren would want – maybe they don't. You likely want to make your passing as easy for your family as possible, which means getting rid of the things you no longer enjoy and those things you can be reasonably sure your family won't want.

Family may want mementos; they may want photographs, even personal things you might have written or crafted, special recipes, and maybe your gardening tools. But they probably do not want your old clothes you no longer wear or that malfunctioning kitchen apparatus.

It is so easy to accumulate STUFF. But you will eventually die like everyone else. Death and taxes, as they say, are the only sure things in life. Your loved ones will most likely be upset and sad when you die. So, make it easier for them.

Does this feel like work instead of a hobby? Maybe for some. But once you get into döstädning, gradually getting rid of things you don't get pleasure from, giving them away, sending them to charity, or throwing them out, you may feel better having freed yourself from clutter. So keep the things you love, and jettison the rest. It's your last gift to your family.

You may find pleasure in going through items hidden away untouched for years. You may feel virtuous when you can give your 'junk' to a charity. You may enjoy giving a surprise gift to a friend.

Death cleaning isn't about dusting and tidying up; it can be seen as a permanent way of organizing your life. It takes courage to face the fact that none of us are immortal. Getting rid of excess allows us to focus on what we appreciate.

SUMMARY

Swedes have found a good life/work balance. Moderation in all things seems to be their standard, and the civilized coffee culture is an excellent example of this. So, too, is the lördagsgodis – a perfect way to have something to look forward to but not to indulge in excess.

'Just enough' links the things Swedes live by, but maybe the sauna is an exception. Death clearing sounds a bit sad but is a way to enjoy the things that matter and to help the people you love after your death.

Lagom
Coffee culture
Lördagsgodis
Sauna
Döstädning

IRELAND (ÉIRE)

The 'Emerald Isle' is green and stunningly beautiful, and the people are full of character.

There has been some confusion about what to call this country. The island is divided – the smaller part, Ulster, in the north, is part of Great Britain. The rest of the island is known as Ireland in English or Éire and is entirely independent.

In 1949, Éire left the Commonwealth and became a republic. The legend tells us that one of the Tuath Dé Danann ('tribe of Gods') named Ernmas had nine children, six of whom were daughters. Three of these became goddesses: Ériu, Banba, and Fódla. Ireland is derived from the name Ériu. In old Irish, this means 'abundant land.'

The land is green, often boggy, with rugged hills and sea cliffs. There are many small islets and inlets on the western shore. It is known to be rainy and misty – hence so green. Dotted around the landscape are archeological treasures, barrows, and ancient castles.

Ireland was Christianised early and produced some of the most beautiful medieval religious books. Around 73% of the population are Catholics today. And Irish pubs are featured worldwide. Sports such as football, golf, and rugby are popular – but Ireland is well known for horse racing and some more local sports like hurling and Gaelic football.

I have chosen five hobbies for you to explore, so let's look at them.

IRISH FAIRIES AND LEPRECHAUNS

Ireland is a land of myths and magic. The soft green of the hills, the crashing Atlantic Ocean on its western shores, and the ever-present myths and legends make Ireland seem a mystical place.

Ireland has its own Gaelic language and Celtic heritage. Keeping the myths alive was an oral tradition. People gathered around the fireside, telling the tales of long ago, perhaps accompanied by a small harp. These tales have been handed down for hundreds of years, almost word for word.

In the 11th century, Irish monks were recording these tales and helping to keep alive the Celtic mythology – Catholicism and 'fairy faith' can co-exist in harmony. The harp of Dagda is just one of many Irish legends. Dagda was a famous warrior and chieftain who owned a magic harp. He was of the tall, golden-haired, and blue-eyed people from the north, suggesting a Viking ancestry.

What else is featured in these tales? Heroes and battles, but also banshees, fairies, and leprechauns. The banshee is a female fairy in both Irish and Scots Gaelic. If you heard the banshee wailing, prepare for the death of a family member.

But perhaps the best-known Irish fairy is the leprechaun. They have various forms and modes of dress. They are generally depicted as small and solitary men bent on mischief. But, dressed in red or green, with a fine beard, they might be shown as shoe-makers, or maybe they have hidden a pot of gold at the end of the rainbow?

One medieval tale tells of King Fergus who fell asleep on the beach. He woke up being dragged into the sea by three leprechauns. He captured them and only let them go in exchange for three wishes.

Various sports teams use leprechauns as mascots – and a wrestler called Dylan Mark Postl competed under the name of a leprechaun called Hornswoggle.

You may not have a leprechaun in your backyard, but there might be local myths and legends that would be interesting to research. If not, why not read about Irish folklore, which is full of adventure, and perhaps you will come to believe in the fairies yourself?

WATERCOLOR PAINTING

Ireland is incredibly beautiful and lends itself to the soft washes of watercolor painting.

Known as the 'Emerald Isle,' one tends to imagine a million shades of green, but when you look and see, you will notice hundreds of blues and other colors. Even in the rain and mist, color and a sense of mystique are part of Ireland's charm.

Because watercolors are transparent, they are often laid down in layers. And if you want a soft, blending effect, then wet-on-wet might be your chosen method. You could use wet-on-dry, dry-on-dry, and dry-on-wet. The paper you use will also affect the finished effect.

There are many videos to demonstrate how to paint watercolors, and looking at the efforts of Irish painters might stimulate you to try your hand. The lovely scenery and delicate colors of Éire have encouraged many people to try capturing some of this island's atmosphere. Watercolor painting is one hobby that is engrossing and can be very satisfying.

SODA BREAD BAKING

Ireland suffered from a devastating potato famine from 1845 to 1849. Soda bread was one alternative food for the poverty-stricken people. Imagine them baking it over their turf fires in their small cottages. It is easy to make, filling, and very tasty.

The Irish eat soda bread for breakfast with jam and a cup of tea. They eat it for lunch with cheese and for dinner with the entrée. But the very best way to eat it is straight from the oven while it is still warm, with salty butter or a big dollop of jam.

What is so special about soda bread? Instead of yeast as the rising agent in soda bread, it uses sodium bicarbonate.

Traditional Irish soda

Traditional soda bread has just four ingredients: flour, baking soda, buttermilk, and salt.

Some modern bakers may add Guinness, orange peel, or other things, but that deviates from the real soda bread, although it may taste delicious.

The taste of the bread comes from the way the baking soda and acidic milk react to form tiny carbon dioxide bubbles in the bread. This gives it a unique texture. And you do not need to knead it, so it is quick to make.

Here is a recipe for you to try:

Ingredients

170 g (6 oz) wholemeal flour and 170 g (6 oz) plain flour
½ tsp salt
½ tsp bicarbonate of soda
290 ml (10 fl oz) buttermilk

Method

- Preheat the oven to 200°C (390°F).
- Put all the dry ingredients in a bowl, make a well in the center, and pour in the buttermilk.
- Mix with a fork to form a soft dough. Adjust the quantity of milk if necessary.
- Turn out onto a floured surface and form into a round shape. Lightly flour a baking sheet and place the slightly-flattened dough on it. Mark a cross on the surface.
- Bake in a hot oven for about 30 minutes.
- It should sound hollow when you tap it. Cool on a wire rack.

Soda bread is delicious. Try it and see! If you are in a hurry and have unexpected guests, this takes about an hour to make and cook and is an unusual and filling offering. Why not make two loaves?

IRISH COMEDY

Irish people have an irresistible sense of humor. It's light, funny, and not offensive.

Often the humor depends upon wordplay and inverted meaning. The punchline will often tell how one person outwits another or confuses him. There is a topsy-turvy logic, which is quite delightful.

When the English imposed their language on the Irish, speaking traditional Irish Gaelic was forbidden, so the Irish people spoke English the Irish way. Unfortunately, many grammatical rules of English are the reverse of Gaelic rules, resulting in an inversion of the language. In addition, any logic was abandoned as being too foolish or abstract for words.

The traditional oral storytellers often had stories with a twist in the tale, which lends itself to modern Irish humor. It can be subtle and only appreciated when you hear the joke delivered in the soft Irish brogue. And nearly all Irish people can tell a funny tale– it seems to come as a natural part of their makeup. Sometimes, you might have to be Irish to 'get it,' though.

Maybe you have a stock of jokes to access when you meet with friends or grandchildren. As a hobby, telling jokes and riddles can be a great way to communicate intergenerationally. They also say that a good belly laugh is one of the very best stress relievers we have.

DUCK HERDING

Dogs herd sheep – yes? But they can also herd other animals - such as ducks. This isn't quite as quaint as it sounds. How else can you put your ducks safely inside a locked pen at night to deprive foxes and other predators?

Some dogs are not much good at herding anything, but others are natural herders. This can be a problem if you are hill walking with your dog and sheep are around. You may think they may be on the next hill, far away, until you see a tiny black and white animal running fast behind a flock of sheep.

Dogs need to be trained for herding, and so do their owners. Some dogs know what a duck looks like, sounds like, and runs like. They recognize the job they have to do in herding the ducks to safety when the farmer commands them to.

A well-trained dog with an aptitude for herding can be taught to herd hens, ducks, and sheep. These dogs need to be gentle, intelligent, and sensitive to the farmer's commands and how the ducks respond. Not all dogs are suitable for duck-herding. But some well-trained dogs do work on a few farms in Ireland.

Watching them spring into action is engaging and quite awe-inspiring.

If you do not have dogs of your own, you can watch them in action at shows or in videos. And if you have a natural couch dog, you can show him too. You might decide to work with your dog to train him in herding. What you can't do is take your dog to the nearest hills and let him or her off the lead and expect them to understand how to act. But it is an entertaining activity to watch.

IRELAND (ÉIRE) | 259

SUMMARY

Ireland might be a small country, but it has stunning scenery and a wide variety of activities to offer. One cannot think about Éire without thinking about legends and myths.

The misty landscape lends itself to the transparent paints of watercolors, and painting is an engrossing hobby with easy access to how-to videos and classes. And if that makes you hungry, soda bread is a fast way to satisfy your appetite. The Irish are funny. Humor is in their genes, and everyone can enjoy a good laugh. Finally, the gentle sport of duck herding – anyone can watch or join in under guidance.

Irish fairies and leprechauns
Watercolor painting
Soda bread baking
Comedy
Duck herding

MONGOLIA

Mongolia is cold and dry. The vast Gobi Desert stretches across large parts of Mongolia and China. The name means "waterless place" in Mongolian. You need strong and tough people to thrive in this harsh climate.

Genghis Khan was a renowned warrior, his hordes sweeping westward across central Asia and southeastward over the Great Wall of China. Today many people still have a nomadic lifestyle – and their hobbies are those needed to survive, like archery or horse and camel racing. Hobbies that are portable and weigh very little such as their wire and ankle bone games are also popular.

These games help pass the frigid winter evenings and involve all ages of the families, who tend to live together in small communities sharing work and play.

They have Naadam, a yearly festival celebrating three traditional games: wrestling, archery, and horse racing. These traditional games are unique, and I have chosen five to represent the variety of Mongolian games and hobbies.

WIRE PUZZLE GAMES

Mongolian puzzle games have been around for a very long time. They were probably played in the Xiongnu, when the Xiongnu were nomads who dominated the Asian steppes, including what is now Mongolia, for over 500 years around the 3rd century BC.

Mongolia has created some of the world's most challenging puzzles and sets. They have nearly 3,000 games of 15 sorts inherited from their ancestors. They are said to help a child's intellectual development.

The games exercise memory, logical thinking, concentration, and problem-solving skills, all needed for the nomadic lifestyle in harsh terrain. There are many puzzle games and variations of wire puzzles.

The golden key wire toy is one such puzzle. This is an iron key ring game. The aim is to unlock as many ring locks without any tools. Sometimes our Christmas crackers may have a small wire escape toy inside – but these are nothing like the complexity of the Mongolian Golden Key.

The puzzles or nail puzzles usually consist of two or more wires tangled up. Closed pieces may include rings or other shapes. So, again, untangle it without cutting the wires or bending them.

These games can be homemade from nails, horseshoes, or any metal. Another variation is a plate and ring puzzle. This has a plate with lots of holes drilled in it and a closed or nearly closed ring that must be disentangled from the plate. You can buy these puzzles with instructions on how to solve them, but they can be complex even with instructions. What a simple yet challenging hobby to work your brain.

ANKLE BONE GAMES

The name for an ankle bone game in Mongolian is 'Shagai,' and there are many, many games played using the ankle bones of goats or sheep. Games similar to dice, games of fortune-telling, and flicking.

These games such as multicolored turtle, flicking, and knucklebones, have strict rules.

One of the most popular games is Alag Malkhii, the multicolored turtle. This game is believed to bring luck to families. According to Buddhist beliefs, the numbers 81 and 108 are lucky, so the number of bones used is 81 or 108.

The bones are painted in five different colors and put in the shape of a turtle (which represents the shape of the Universe). Then, players roll the dice and collect the bones to make their own little turtle. The winner is the player who has created the most turtles when all the bones have been used.

You will be glad to know that the bones are cleaned and polished before use. The bones have four sides, although they are naturally irregular. I am not sure what your local butcher would make of a request for ankle bones, but you can buy sets of them. Working out the ways to play would be an interesting and unusual hobby.

BUILD YOUR OWN YURT

You can build your own yurt, any size, from a miniature toy to a live-in tent size. The yurt is the Mongolian prefabricated and removable house – a luxurious tent with windows and door frames.

The traditional yurt is called a "ger" and differs only in the roof construction. They have been in existence for over 300 years, so they are much tested. As a nomadic house, the yurts are quick to erect and withstand the winds. They are light to carry and essential since Mongolian nomads tended to move locations four or more times a year.

Building your own yurt, whether it be a miniature model or a nearly full size, helps us to understand a little of the culture of these unique nomadic people. Many are highly decorated and beautifully constructed. You can buy kits of all sizes for your grandchildren and yourself. Model yurt building would make an informative and unusual hobby.

ARCHERY

Archery in Mongolia has an important place in past legends and history. Erekhe Mergen was a famous archer. When there was a terrible drought, he saved the people by shooting down no less than six suns.

The legendary 'Mother of Mongolia' wanted to make peace between her aggressive sons. So she gave each son an arrow and told them to break it. That was easy! Then she gave each son a bunch of six arrows and told them to snap it – and they couldn't. The lesson? In unity is strength.

Then came Genghis Khan and his horde of Huns sweeping across vast areas of Asia, with their hardy mares and bows, cutting down all in their path. The bows of Genghis Khan were smaller than modern bows but very effective. Did you know that his military conquests were not the only way Genghis Khan imprinted his fame on the world? It is said that there are 16 million men who might be directly descended from him! They have the same Y chromosome.

Archery was essential to the Mongolian nomadic life to obtain food. Children grew up learning to use the bow and arrow from a young age. Archery is still a popular hobby, and there are Mongolian archery festivals. These are colorful affairs with hundreds of white gers and multicolored tents spread across the ground. The composite bow can take a long time to create from natural materials.

Archery is a hobby that we can all enjoy – although the Mongolian method might be hard to emulate.

DEMBEE

Dembee is a finger game with elements of chanting, visual acuity, and manual dexterity.

The idea is to guess the number of fingers two players are displaying. But the game is fast and furious. The fingers move quickly, so you must respond at speed – in a sing-song manner – cantillating. Every time you score, you press one finger on one hand, and the first to reach the fifth finger wins.

The penalty for losing is to drink fermented (sour) milk.

This game tests all your senses – vision, hearing, response speed, fingers' agility, and even taste if you lose. So, you guess and tell, almost like a musical debate. To make it more demanding, the fingers have names such as 'Spick one' and 'seven Domboo.'

This is a demanding game, and variations in how the fingers are shown, or the melodies used, make it constantly exciting and testing.

Dembee is a traditional game derived from the ancient custom of starting to milk the mares at the beginning of summer and making fermented milk. And anyone can play – young or old, man or woman. But every loser must drink the 'airag' to the bottom of the cup. Otherwise, severe weather would follow. They even have a special bowl for drinking the airag – and the fermented mare's milk has many medicinal properties.

To play Dembee, you would need to watch, either on video or, if lucky, the real experience. One advantage of this game is that you need nothing except your acute senses to play - except the airag.

SUMMARY

Mongolia has a significant number of unique games suited to its nomadic lifestyle and harsh climate. It is a fascinating country, and playing their games helps us understand a little about their lives.

Wire Puzzles Games
Anklebone Games
Build your Own Yurt
Archery
Dembee

SOUTH KOREA

South Koreans know how to work hard and play hard. The working week was reduced from 68 hours maximum to 52 hours in 2018, giving people more opportunities to enjoy their hobbies.

The most popular hobbies for South Koreans concern fitness and sport (34%), according to a survey carried out in 2019. This was followed by learning a foreign language (28%) and learning how to invest in third (24%).

Some of the sports enjoyed include badminton, football, baseball, and traditional martial arts like Taekwondo and judo – the former being extremely energetic, with kicks and fast movements taking a lifetime to become proficient. Many South Koreans are now taking up fencing and enjoying its competitiveness.

South Korea has some beautiful natural parks to explore. Of course, music plays an integral part in social life. But learning a foreign language, very often English, is seen as almost essential with the increased use of the internet and social media.

Let's dive into the most popular hobbies a South Korean is likely to partake in.

HIKING

Hiking is a popular hobby in South Korea – and there is good reason for this. The countryside is gorgeous, and the hardworking people of South Korea likely crave a change of scenery for some mental relaxation.

Apart from the green hilly countryside, cherry trees, and ancient Buddhist temples, there are sub-tropical islands to explore and the coastline with its fishing villages.

The Seoraksan National Park has been a UNESCO Biosphere Protection site since 1982. Covering 63 square miles, it has many places to discover. There are lovely mountains like

Seoraksan Mountain, or 'Snowy Mountain,' reaching 5,604 ft high. Beautiful mountain trails and stunning scenery, including steep cliffs, waterfalls, and caves.

The Sinheunga is reputed to be the oldest Seon temple in the world. Surrounding the temple complex are around 200 pools. And if animals interest you, there are otters, flying squirrels, maybe a black bear, and if you are fortunate, you might catch a glimpse of the rare Korean musk deer or Korean goral.

There are national parks and pleasant countryside near most of us – and the thing is - when we live in a particular place, we are less likely to hike around and explore the natural wonders near home. So why not list the spectacular sites nearby and take the time to hike and explore locally?

FOLK MUSIC

In 1145, the history of the three kingdoms described two string-like instruments. Music reflected the social hierarchy. The elite classes used orthodox music, usually played in ceremonies, banquets, and military processions. And then there was the people's music, which included folk songs, becoming increasingly respected as the traditional music of South Korea.

Pansori, meaning 'the place where many people gather,' originated in the 17th century – perhaps derived from the shamanic narrative song. Pansori music contains percussion and a solo singer, the contemporary music of South Korea. Pungmul Nori is percussion music with dominant drums and is considered traditional music. Folk songs varied from region to region.

When Japan overcame the Korean peninsula in 1895, they imposed a European style of music, but this was less accessible to the poorer classes, and they maintained their traditional style of music. For example, you may know the song, 'Oh, my darling Clementine?' This derives from the modern Ch'angga, which in turn comes from Pansori. So as you can see, South Korean music has a complex past and combines traditional Korean music and ballads with Western styles. And now we have 'K-pop' with large boy bands who sing and dance. This may or may not be your style, but it is undoubtedly easy to sing along with.

Folk music is a music style still found worldwide and has quite the following, with folk festivals cropping up all over the place. If you enjoy this music and are drawn to this sound, why not make a hobby of it. Listening to it or picking up an instrument like a guitar and creating your own folk songs are great choices.

FENCING

The number one hobby for South Koreans is keeping physically fit with a sports activity, and the most up-and-coming sport is fencing.

South Korean fencers have won five gold medals, three silver, and eight bronze medals in Olympic fencing as of the time of writing – and alongside China, this is the most for any Asian country.

The men's saber team have interesting names: 'The Terminator,' 'The Legend,' and 'The Sonic.' One is left-handed, which must have its advantages. Their leader is number eight in the world ranking. This is an exceptional achievement since fencing has been a European sport until quite recently.

Gaining in popularity in South Korea, you will be able to note the progression of South Korea in fencing, and it is a fun sport to watch with its grace and fast moves.

Maybe there is a team near you or a club you could participate in? Fencing is a sport open to men and women – and while a specific strength and dexterity are needed, it also depends upon strategy. It could be compared to a physical form of chess.

Fencing would be quite a demanding sport, but if you are reasonably fit, it gives an excellent workout for the body and the brain at any age.

FOREIGN LANGUAGE LEARNING

Learning a foreign language is the second most popular leisure-time activity in South Korea, and it is also one suggested method to stave off dementia.

In Korea, the most common foreign language learned is English (the language of business.) Mandarin and Japanese are also in demand. South Koreans are very competitive, and speaking English is one way to advance. Entrance to Universities demands a high proficiency in English, plus the fact that much of the internet language is predominantly English.

And how about you?

If you want to learn a new language do you want to become proficient quickly, do you want a real challenge, or have you some practical purpose in mind?

To help you make up your mind, here are some 'easier' languages for English speakers:

Norwegian has many similar words, straightforward grammar, and so many local accents that you don't need to worry about pronunciation.

Spanish also has many similar words and is easy to pronounce (and the second most spoken language in the world.)

Dutch and **Portuguese** are relatively easy, as is Indonesian. However, unlike most Asian languages, Indonesian uses the Latin alphabet. And unlike English, you pronounce it how it is spelled.

Italian is a language where you add an 'o' or an 'a' to the ends of English words and hope for the best. Italians are marvelous at sign language.

Now for the real challenges for English speakers:

Mandarin is the most widely spoken native language in the world. Their writing system is quite different from the Latin alphabet, and the tonal quality of the speech affects the meaning of words. One example is the word 'ma.' It can mean horse, scold, rough, or mother, just according to what tone you use to say it.

Arabic is another language that is very hard to learn for English speakers. There are so many variants, so where do you start? There are 28 letters, but often the vowels are omitted, and they write from right to left.

So how will you choose which language to learn?

SUMMARY

South Koreans have enormous energy and enthusiasm for work and play.

Hiking in their incredible natural parks enables them to relax, find a sense of peace, and be one with nature, and the scenery is exciting and varied. Fencing is an activity you may not have thought of taking part in. Music seems to be common to all cultures as old as humankind. But if you want to give your brain a workout, try learning a foreign language.

Hiking
Folk Music
Fencing
Learning a Foreign Language

TURKEY

Turkey is unique. It lies in Asia and Europe, with a bridge and a barrier.

The land is mostly mountainous, with dramatic cliffs and high summits. Mount Ararat is 16,945 feet (5,165 meters) high. There are climatic contrasts between the high interior and the coastal areas, marked by summer droughts and harsh snowy winters.

Turkey is full of natural wonders and man-made historical buildings and architectural sites. For example, Istanbul has the stunning Byzantine Hagia Sophia Mosque. One of the world's most beautiful buildings and the largest church for over 1,000 years. And not far away is the sumptuous Topkapı Palace, the palace of the sultans and their harems.

Ephesus has a tremendous archeological interest, mighty Roman ruins, and roads with marble columns. Natural wonders include the rocky valleys of Cappadocia, together with the churches and homes cut into the rock.

But for hobbies, I have found ones that people enjoy when they are not working or sightseeing, and we will start with the cats.

CATS AND TURKS

When you visit Turkey, you will see many, many cats. It has been estimated that Istanbul has possibly over a million feral cats. You may find cats sitting on the bus, on the ferry, in the subway, in cafes, and on the street.

Why is this?

Turkey has a policy of not hurting or capturing these cats. They are seen as communal pets rather than unwanted strays.

When the Ottomans settled in Istanbul, most houses were made of wood and harbored rats and mice, so cats were valuable. Cats are also very clean animals. In addition, if you look at a cat's forehead, you can see above both eyes an "M" shape, said to be a sign that Muhammad blessed the cats, or so it is said by some.

But it does mean cats have a long and respected history in Turkey.

In Istanbul, there are vending machines for cats and dogs. People can put in a few coins as they pass by, and the money is used to feed cats and dogs. It seems a very humane way of dealing with these animals.

Even if you don't have a rat or mouse problem, a cat can be a wonderful pet if you are prepared to serve it and accept that your cat might be in charge. Having a cat can be a fun hobby, especially if you surround yourself with other cat owners, talking about all things cats.

BACKGAMMON

Backgammon is immensely popular in Turkey. Everyone seems to understand the game, which they call 'tavla.' If you visit Turkey, you will see backgammon boards out everywhere. Cafes, tea gardens, on the pavements, and every Turkish sailing boat, the gulet, will have one or more backgammon sets. And, of course, every household owns at least one set.

To play tavla well, you need skill and a measure of luck. The game is addictive as you learn the subtleties of playing well. Usually, this game is played extremely fast; the faster you play, the more skilled you are considered to be.

Although the game is vocal, Turkish people count the numbers where the dice rolls in their heads, not out loud.

Backgammon is the world's oldest board game, originating in Mesopotamia thousands of years ago. As a result, many Turks know the numbers 1-6 in Farsi, which may be the only words they know in Persian.

You may find that backgammon is a very talkative game with players talking through their proposed moves and their consequences. It's a great way for strangers to meet up and play with an audience who also participates in verbal exchanges.

The game reflects the uncertainties in life – how will the dice roll? How best can you play on? So, why not set up a backgammon board and challenge your neighbor to a match, preferably with an audience and a nice cup of Turkish tea.

RUMMIKUB OR OKEY

Rummikub or Okey is a very popular game in Turkey. It originates in Germany, but Turkish expatriates and people living in Turkey enjoy playing Rummikub or Okey, which is similar.

Cafes and bars will often have a game of Okey running. The suggestion is that anyone over eight years can play, so it's an easy way for generations to mix in fun yet competitive ways. Usually, there are 2-4 players, but one can play online, with friends or family, or with people in far-off places around the world. It would be one way of keeping in touch when relatives have moved away. You can also pit yourself against computer opponents.

The game is a mixture of Mah-jong and rummy; it uses 104 tiles, which they call cubes, and draws many of the rules from rummy. So, it is easy to learn and involves grouping and ordering the cubes to make runs, just like the cards in rummy.

The cubes are numbered one to thirteen, and instead of suites, they are colored black, yellow, red, or blue, equivalent to two decks of cards. Each player starts with 14 tiles, and the player with the highest number starts the game.

Rummikub is said to benefit the brain because the hippocampus and prefrontal cortex, associated with memory and complex thought processes, are stimulated.

Okey or Rummikub is easy to play and makes a change from card or board games. If you want a sociable game with your friends or a solo computer challenge, then Rummikub might be a good choice.

OLIVE OIL SOAP MAKING

Soap is said to have been invented about 5,000 years ago in ancient Babylon. In Roman times, animal fats were used, but the Arabs and Persians produced the first soaps using vegetable oils in medieval times.

Olive oil soap has been made in Turkey since the 16th century. Because olive oil is abundant in the region, large soap-making enterprises evolved and now produce a wide range of enchanting soaps.

Turkish olive oil soap retains the natural ingredients, consisting of olive oil, salt – and natural scents like rose, thyme, lavender, and chamomile. In Istanbul or Izmir, the soap is presented naturally – large blocks on hay or straw; the blocks can be cut down to order. They are olive-green, white, or off-white. And the nice thing is that the olive oil soap is very inexpensive.

Fortunately, you can buy Turkish soap in many countries, and the natural feel and organic basis are becoming increasingly sought after. Olive oil soap is said to be good for the skin and strengthening the hair.

It is possible to make olive oil soap at home – and a bar of natural health-giving olive oil soap would make fine gifts and benefit yourself.

TEA & COFFEE – TURKISH STYLE

Tea

Turkey is one of the top 5 tea-growing countries globally, producing up to 10% of the total global production. And over half will be drunk by the Turks themselves.

The eastern Black Sea coast is full of tea farms; the mild climate, fertile soil, and plentiful rain make this an ideal growing area for tea. During the 5th century, tea was imported to Turkey via the Silk Road. Still, the boost to its popularity came when the Ottoman Empire fell after WW1, Turkey lost the coffee-producing areas, and coffee became very expensive. The country leader - Atatürk – encouraged tea drinking as a substitute.

Turks make tea in their own way. Two stacked kettles are used. The top is smaller, with the tea steeping in it for about 10 minutes, and the lower kettle has boiling water so that the tea drinker can dilute the tea to his or her taste. The tea is served in glass vessels, a cube of sugar is added, and the drinker holds the glass by its brim to avoid burning its fingertips. (Never add milk or lemon!)

Coffee

Turkish coffee is strong, though not as strong as espresso. When served in Turkey, they also serve a glass of water to clear your palette. While sipping the water, the fine coffee grounds will sink to the bottom of the cup.

The coffee is unfiltered so never stir it, or the 'mud' which sinks to the bottom of the glass will swirl around in the drink. The coffee is finely ground and often served with a small, sweet biscuit or sweet such as Turkish delight.

The coffee itself will often have sugar added to its preparation. Sometimes cardamon, a powerful antioxidant, will also be added to the coffee. You do not have to drink the silt at the bottom of the cup, but if you see someone turning the cup over after drinking, they may be telling their fortune from the pattern left by the dregs in the cup.

If you are lucky enough to have Turkish friends, they will probably be delighted to share their secrets of making tea or coffee the Turkish way. But if you do not know any Turkish people, you can still try your hand at making tea or coffee in perhaps a somewhat different way.

Invite your neighbor and get chatting over Turkish tea or coffee. It could be a great ice-breaker.

SUMMARY

Turkey has so much to offer, including incredible and varied scenery, archeology, and stunning buildings, but what do the people who live among such splendors do in their spare time? Turkey has many fun hobbies, from their love of cats to board games to making olive oil soaps. And finally, tea and coffee Turkish style. What better way to spend a few hours chatting with friends and family.

Cats and Turks
Backgammon
Rummikub or Okey
Olive Oil Soap Making
Tea and coffee Turkish style

OMAN

Oman is a small country with spectacular scenery, deserts, mountains, and the sea. The people of Oman have a long history and create beautiful crafts displayed in some of the best souks in the world.

The countryside is speckled with castles, forts, and tiny villages hidden in the mountains. There are isolated beaches, and the weather has hot sunshine for the sun worshippers, together with rains for the lush green countryside. Diving centers, water sports, and wild sea-life observation are hobbies enjoyed in Oman.

I have tried to find hobbies you can take on, in your own community. But nothing could beat the experience of a voyage into Oman, to meet the people firsthand, immerse yourself in a souk, and perhaps camp out under the stars under the clear desert skies.

WADI FUN – RIVERBED HIKING AND SWIMMING

Oman has a great variety of different terrains. Inland are craggy mountains, deserts, and wadis.

The wadis are dry riverbeds and make for exciting and interesting hikes. The possibility of flash floods no doubt adds to the excitement. So guides who understand the area and the weather not only add to the interest of the trip but also ensure the safety of the party.

The wadis can provide strenuous walking, so hiking boots are essential, as is carrying water. But the scenery is stunning! The wadi may be dry and arid but also feature natural springs and pools of water, reflecting the turquoise sky. Cooling off in the clear waters is an added charm.

Sloshing along a not-quite-dry wadi is a marvelous way to get the exercise we all need. In addition, wadis and rivers often have history embedded in their makeup. Water is where people have made their homes since the earliest of times. Every river, every stream has its stories to tell.

In Oman, away from the crowded cities of the coastal regions, you can find cliff-top villages where time seems to have stood still. You might discover irrigated terraces, date farms – and perhaps orchards of the rare frankincense tree.

Now, you may not have a wadi at your back door – but you may perhaps have a stream or a river? Following the bank of your local river can be an adventure of discovery.

There are plants, grasses, and trees. Do you know all of them? If you are lucky, there may be fauna to watch, water holes and fish in the water, frogs halfway between land and water, shy deer, badgers, otters, beavers, or foxes, and riverbanks are often teeming with birdlife both on and off the water.

In addition to the natural wonders of the riverbank, there may be history. The more you look into the past, the more fascinating it becomes. Who lived here? Have they left any traces? Are there documents to tell us a little about the people who made this place their home? In Oman, you can follow a Wadi, but you can explore a nearby stream or river back home.

SOUK MARKET EXPLORATION

If you like shopping, then you would love the Omani Souk. They seem to sell everything, much of it handcrafted and often unique.

One of the oldest marketplaces in the world is the Souk of Muttrah, which can get very crowded. The colors, the scents, the calls of the merchants, and the vibrancy of life here, are so full of energy. It would be easy to spend a day just looking around.

You will find Omani pottery used for storing dates and grains, as water bottles, and frankincense burners simply for decoration. Palm leaf woven baskets and textiles in every color are just some things you can see on display.

How well have you explored your local market? Are there nearby ones you could compare it with? Market visits are an engaging hobby for many people, and they usually come home with something interesting to add to their collection.

SILVERSMITHING

Some of the loveliest crafts you can find in the souk is the silverware. Ancient jewelry is rare since when a woman dies, her jewelry is melted to form new pieces for her daughters. The original Omani silverware was made from Marie Theresa dollars (Thalers), the only source of silver in Oman. In Austria, these were minted in 1789, and Europeans brought them to Oman. This silver is smooth and silky to feel.

Silversmithing is a hobby that anyone can do – you don't need Thalers, and you can produce your own style of jewelry. You may need to attend classes to get started. But taken step by step, it is not too difficult. Sawing, then filing, are the first two steps. Then comes the forging, hammering, and making your piece into your desired shape.

It might be a good idea to practice on copper, which looks nice but is cheaper than silver. Soldering comes next, and then you can add the finishing touches, and voila – a unique item made by you. This might sound difficult, and maybe for some, it is.

But this hobby is immensely rewarding for the individual who wants to learn this craft.

HALAWET AHMAD DESSERT MAKING

Omani foods are full of flavor. They use spices and colors and decorate their dishes with nuts and fruits, both savory and desserts.

Shuma 'The National Dish' is a roast using lamb, goat meat, or perhaps beef or camel. The meat is coated with a mix of spices, including cardamon, cumin, cloves, chili peppers, and coriander.

Many of their dishes are rice-based, such as chicken kabouli. A similar blend of spices livens up this dish, usually garnished with dates, chickpeas, sultanas, and nuts.

If you have a sweet tooth, you might like to try Halawet Ahmad, a traditional Omani dessert. To make it, combine roasted vermicelli (you can use colored vermicelli to make it more interesting) with condensed milk, desiccated coconut, butter, and almond powder. In Oman, the mixture is served as molded dome shapes and decorated with pistachios or almonds.

Here is one recipe for Halawet Ahmad:

Ingredients

1 cup butter
400 g vermicelli
1 tin sweetened condensed milk
1 cup almond powder

1 cup desiccated coconut

Method

- Sauté the vermicelli noodles in the butter until golden. Then add the condensed milk, almond powder, and coconut.
- Heat gently, stirring for 2 minutes. Let it cool a little, then transfer to molds.
- When it has cooled, it is ready to decorate and serve.

Once you have tried this out, it might become a popular, quick, and easy dessert to prepare. Making desserts might not be the healthiest hobby, but what if you turned it into a dessert club or for passive income by selling your desserts to a local restaurant?

BASKET WEAVING

Think of Oman, and you think of palm trees. They are everywhere. And Omanis don't just eat the dates; they also use palm leaves to make mukhraf and murbah - bags to collect the dates and intricately woven shoulder bags.

They also make baskets to store grain and dates or cook meat. Weaving palm fronds is an ancient Omani craft. They make furniture, mats, and coverings for food to protect it from insects.

The craft seemed to be dying out when four girls resurrected the palm leaf industry to produce a range of items, including luggage, storage boxes, dishes, and more.

Weaving is a hobby that has many variations depending on the type of material used, the colors, and patterns, the weave itself, and the range of finished products. For example, many hobbyists use willow bands to weave their baskets; others use textiles to make mats and rugs. In Oman, they use palm leaves.

If you are interested in trying it out, there are often classes you can attend, videos to watch, and DIY books to read. I bet that sitting in the sunshine weaving a beautiful basket is a very relaxing hobby.

SUMMARY

Oman has stunning scenery and many beautiful crafts. You can take inspiration from these, even though you may not have a Wadi in your backyard or a local market like a souk.

Weaving and silversmithing are both hobbies you can adapt to your own needs. Both can enable you to produce unique items which will give years of pleasure. Likewise, dessert-making can be very tasty and rewarding.

Wadi Fun - Riverbed Hiking and Swimming
Souk Market Explorations
Silversmithing
Halawet Ahmad Dessert
Basket Weaving

SCOTLAND

Scotland is a small country to the north of England and is part of the United Kingdom. Famously separated by the Roman Wall, named after Emperor Hadrian, the border areas have long been conflicted.

Scotland is mainly mountainous, with long sea lochs indenting the coast. The country is beautiful, sometimes remote, and wild. Dotted with fortified towers or peels and castles, you are never far from the history of this country. The Scottish people have held onto many traditional ways and the musical Scottish dialect.

One thinks of highland kilts and claymores, mists and mountains, lonely bothies, and sleepy fishing villages. Yet Scotland has contributed to explorers and adventurers all over the world, inventions we use every day, and culinary delights such as the haggis and the deep-fried mars bar.

I have picked out five hobbies you might enjoy but have a look at a recording of the highland games for a sense of Scotland today.

THE HOBBY

The hobby is a bird. It is about the size of a kestrel and visits Scotland between April to September. But it is rare and only restricts itself to a few sites. During the winter months, they live in Africa.

The hobby has a fine black 'mustache,' smart red 'trousers,' and long pointed wings like a large swift. The legs are yellow, as are their short chunky beaks. The feathers are black and tan, grey, orange, and white. So, they are smartly turned out.

This bird hunts on the wing and catches large insects, like dragonflies, small birds, like swallows, and bats. They often catch their prey with their sharp talons and transfer it to their beaks in flight.

They have been known to steal from other birds, such as kestrels. And their flight is a true aerobatic display. Very fast, very maneuverable, and very agile. Studying a rare bird allows one to become an expert, and the more you find out, the more engrossing they are. Beautiful masters of the air, what isn't there to like?

BURNS NIGHT

A Scottish Burns night is something to remember and treasure. Everyone dresses for the celebration. The women in long skirts, often tartan, a blouse, and maybe a tartan sash, held with a Clan brooch. But the men – ahh, the men – dressed in full glory in their tartan kilts, their dirks stuck in their socks, and their sporrans. The sporran takes the place of pockets and can be quite decorative.

Burns suppers are held all over Scotland and in many foreign countries. It's a celebration of the birthday of Scotland's national poet, Robert (Robbie) Burns. And there is a certain formality in the supper, but here is a typical example:

> After the guests have taken their places, a procession takes place. Leading the procession is a piper playing the bagpipes as the haggis is piped in. The chief cook proudly bears the haggis on a large tray. This is laid reverently before the host. The host then exclaims the famous 'Address to the Haggis,' often ending it with a mighty blow from his sword to make the first cut in the haggis. Everyone toasts the haggis.
>
> Then comes the meal. Haggis served with neeps and tatties. (Neeps can be turnip or swede, and tatties are potatoes – mashed.) It actually tastes good, especially with the natural Scottish accompaniment of real Scottish whiskey.
>
> After dining, the main speech, the 'Immortal Memory,' is given. Then, there is a Toast to the Lassies and a Reply. Other entertainment may be provided by the guests who perform some of the bard's poems and songs. These can be delivered in quite a fearsome style.
>
> To end the evening, the host gives a 'Toast of Thanks,' and then everyone stands up, links crossed arms, and

sings Robby Burns' poem, 'Auld lang Syne.' (Note that the high road means the highway, but the low road means death.)

You can buy haggis for vegans and kosher haggis, but Americans cannot import the real haggis from Scotland.

There is nothing quite like a Burns night. It would take a lot of work to organize one, but it could be done, especially if friends join in the preparations. Of course, you would need a piper, a haggis, a few kilts, and a sword. But ending with Auld Lang Syne would make a Burns night a night to remember.

THE HIGHLAND FLING

The highland fling is a traditional dance of Scotland. It probably originated in the 17th century as a solo man's victory dance after a battle, usually against the English.

The dance is vigorous, precise, and athletic. Watching the dance helped the clan chiefs choose the most robust and disciplined men for battle.

Sometimes the precise movements are danced between the crossed blades of two swords. The 'fling' relates to how the dancer flings his (or her leg) behind or in front while hopping from one leg to the other. The dance is done with speed and lightness to the sound of the bagpipes.

The steps are intricate, and the order for the annual competitions may change. The dance is in 4/4 time, but the time has slowed from 192 beats per minute a hundred years ago to the present 114 bpm (which is still pretty fast!)

Watching the highland fling with the bagpipes wailing and the swirling kilts of the dancers is evocative of earlier times. You need to be fit to undertake this dance seriously, but there are videos to show you how if you fancy dressing up and trying it out. If the highland fling is too much for you, other Scottish dances are easier for the less fit.

GURNING

Gurning is an unusual sport and requires a strong sense of humor. It relates to pulling grotesque faces, traditionally through a horse harness.

In English, the word 'gurn' means "to snarl, to look savage," while in Scotland, the word means 'grin,' and the Irish use 'gurnin' to cry. Once a year, the gurning championship is held in Egremont, in northwest England, and close to the Scottish border, in their Crab Fair.

The rules are strict, no plastic teeth, no padding, or any other accessories. The winner is the man or woman who makes the most significant transformation of their face. Also, it makes for a great workout since you have 42 facial muscles.

You might try this north-of-England and Scottish hobby. We all pull faces from time to time, but who amongst your friends can pull the most distorted, terrifying face? Is it you?

HOME BEER BREWING

Scotland is renowned for its whiskey, with different areas having their own unique taste due to the water locally available. But distilling spirits is illegal in the UK, so many Scots have taken to brewing beer, and they find this a very satisfying hobby, as do their friends.

The start-up cost is not inconsiderable, and there is a steep learning curve, but once you have got into your beer brewing, it can become fascinating, and you are always learning new facts and experimenting to get the best results.

Beer-brewing is a very ancient hobby. Many home beer brewers start out using relatively cheap kits that are readily available. But there are some facts to consider before splashing out.

You need to ask yourself some questions before you start:

- Do you have room for the kit?
- Would you be devastated if your batch fails as they sometimes do?
- To begin with, it can be expensive, although it might save you money in the long run.

So why brew your own beer? It can be fun; you learn something all the time, a piece of history, a new recipe, etc. You make friends both in learning and in sampling the product. You can make your own unique tasting beer. There is a lot of help out there as the hobby of home beer making is becoming more and more popular. Sharing your experience on forums and reading other people's blogs is all out there, just waiting to be found.

SUMMARY

Scotland is a beautiful country with generous, strong, and inventive people.

The hobby is a bird, and as its name states, it must be part of this book. It illustrates the rare and robust colors and behavior suited to Scotland. Then we come to Burns Night. This is a part of a tradition in Scotland and is like no other ceremony.

If you want to keep fit, Scotland offers two somewhat different approaches, the highland fling, and gurning. Finally, after a hectic day gurning, why not settle down to your own home-brewed beer. You will have earned it.

The Hobby
Burns Night
Highland Fling
Gurning
Home Beer Brewing

CHILE

Chile is long and thin, with various climates, natural features, and traditions in different parts of this extraordinary country.

The name 'Chile' from the indigenous Aymara means 'Where the land ends.'

Chile has the driest desert in the world – the Atacama. Some places have had no rain since records began. When it does rain, fields of purple flowers stretch for miles. The highest volcano is in Chile at 22,615 feet and is active. The Chinchorro mummies are the oldest in the world, dating from around 5,050 BC. According to the Guinness Book of World Records, they also have their largest swimming pool.

Another record Chile holds is the largest earthquake ever recorded – 9.5 on the Richter Scale, which occurred in 1960 near Valdivia. It lasted a terrifying 11-13 minutes and killed over 1,000 people. In addition, Chile has roughly 3,000 volcanoes, about 36 of them active.

From this fascinating country, I have pulled out five hobbies you might like to try at home – one of them is not mummy making.

CHILEAN MUSIC

Music is enjoyed by over 60% of the population in Chile and is the number one hobby. Music existed in South America long before the Europeans came, and some aspects of this early music remain in Chilean Music. Then there is the Music of the Spanish conquistadors and modern music up to the present day.

Archaeologists have excavated many musical instruments from even the pre-Inca time. Complex musical systems with minor intervals, chromaticism, and scales with five, six, seven, or eight notes were in vogue, similar to other cultures in Asia and Europe.

In some areas of Chile, people still speak and sing songs in the ancient Cunza language. Later, music was to honor the gods, and modern music still retains elements of this culture. However, Christianity absorbed and added new favors, and now jazz and rock have been added to the musical mix.

You can buy local instruments such as the Trutruca (a kind of trumpet that incorporates a cattle horn to amplify the sound) or maybe a Pingkullwe (a transverse flute with five holes), a Huada (a rattle made from a pumpkin with small pebbles or seeds inside) and many other instruments.

The music varies just like the Chilean landscape changes from north to south. Still, now it has a national identity, and almost everyone loves to make music: rap or opera, orchestral or individual, there is something for everyone.

Folk music tended to be disregarded until governmental reforms in the 1960s and the New Chilean Songs movement emerged—this preserved Chilean traditions, from songs to recipes to proverbs. Then in 1973 came the military coup, and music suffered a significant setback like other forms of culture. But in the 1990s, the military regime ended, and music was reborn.

The variety of music in Chile is impressive. There are many instruments unfamiliar to other parts of the world. But whatever your taste in music is, as Kahlil Gibran wrote, "Music is the language of the spirit. It opens the secret of life bringing peace, abolishing strife."

What could be better than that?

FLAGS AND THEIR STORIES

The knowledge of flags can lead you to all sorts of historical facts, facts about battles, the way people thought when they drew up the flags, and the importance they might play in the lives of the citizens.

The Chilean flag has a horizontal divider, the top half white and the bottom half red. On the top corner of the hoist side is a blue square and a single white star in the square.

The colors come from the time when Chile was struggling for independence. White denotes the snow from the snowy peaks of the high Andes; blue represents the sky, and red, the bloodshed during the fight for independence. Added to these representations are the colors derived from the Chilean Indians – white for unity and freedom and the five points for the five provinces the country was originally divided into.

Every flag has a story to tell, whether it is the country's flag, more local, a festival or company, or a sport. Collecting images of them and discovering why they are as they are could provide you with hours of study, entertainment, and a lovely memento.

CHILEAN ICE CREAM (AND OTHER DESSERTS)

Chileans eat more ice cream than people in any other Latin American country, but they have some other fantastic desserts as well.

The desserts range from decadent cakes to cookie sandwiches to roasted milk. Let's look at some of them in more detail to whet your appetite.

Alfajores are the 'Chilean Oreos' – two round shortbread cookies sandwiching a spread, usually made from sugar and boiled milk. Coated with chocolate, desiccated coconut, or left plain, it's a treat.

Leche Asada or 'Roasted milk' – This decadent dessert is a rich mixture of eggs, sugar, and vanilla, in a flan case. The surface of Leche Asada is a crispy, toasted custard layer cooked separately in a hot water bath.

Leche Nevada or 'Floating Islands' – This popular dessert is egg-based; white, frothy meringue islands are floating on it. In Chile, the Leche Nevada is served in a small glass, and you eat it with a coffee spoon. This sweet dessert is straightforward to make and can be whipped up in less than ten minutes.

Torta de Mil Hojas or 'Cake of 1,000 leaves' – The leaves are thin puff pastry layers stacked high. Between them are manjar and walnuts. 'Manjar' is a sweet sauce, similar to caramel, with a smooth, rich flavor. Sometimes an acidic jam is added to counteract the richness of the manjar. This rich cake is often served at birthday parties or baptisms.

Cocadas – Simple and sweet, just eggs and desiccated coconut shaped into balls. If you need gluten-free desserts – then this is safe and simple.

Chilean Ice Cream – Chilean ice cream is exceptional. Here you can find flavors that are unique to Chile. Maybe the fruit used only grows in South America, such as eggfruit and custard apple. Carob is another popular flavor, and plants like Rica and chañar may flavor the ice cream.

You can easily make ice cream and find unique flavors that delight you. Sounds like a delicious hobby to take up.

POETRY COMPOSING

Chile is known as the 'country of poets.' Two Chilean poets have won Nobel prizes for literature.

Gabriela Mistral's passion was education and literature. She wanted to help others as she had experienced a childhood of poverty since her father abandoned his family when she was only three years old.

She empathized with the Indigenous Mapuche women who were badly treated, writing a sad poem ('Poems of the Saddest

Mother') based on their experiences. She set up evening classes for the workers and gave voice to the women who, at the time, were not heard.

As a Nobel laureate, she worked at a girls' school when Pablo Neruda was a teenager, publishing poems and articles for the local paper, and she encouraged him.

Pablo Neruda became not only a renowned poet but also a diplomat and left-wing politician. He wrote his poems in green ink. To him, that symbolized hope and longing. He published his first book before he was twenty and the hugely successful 'Twenty Love Poems and a Song of Despair' soon after.

Chile has many other illustrious poets. The harsh landscape and political instability have provided a background for them, but maybe you have feelings inside you to express in poetry? The economy of words and the poem's rhythm make writing poetry a wonderful way to release your energy and maybe inspire others. Some of the Chilean poets are worth reading to give you ideas for your own efforts.

UFO HUNTING

Do you believe in UFOs and Aliens?

As our explorations lead us deeper and deeper into space, we find worlds out there that might support life. So is it unrealistic to suggest that alien life has visited us?

If you want to see an Unidentified Flying Object (UFO), then Chile is the place to go. And, so far, we cannot explain everything we have seen in the night sky. The night sky of Chile is clear and dark. Pollution is minimal, and they have fine observatories in high places to peer through the atmosphere deep into space.

Many recorded sightings have occurred, including the 'Chilean Roswell' of 1998. Several witnesses thought a UFO crashed into a hill, and so convinced were they that special envoys from NASA and the Chilean army investigated and decided not to make their findings known.

Chile has an official UFO research bureau. It is part of the Air Force's duty to monitor unusual aircraft activity. "Watching the skies" is a popular Chilean hobby, with social media posts to back up their findings.

UFOs are often confused with airplanes, satellites, Chinese lanterns, and even meteorites. So how can you tell if it's a real UFO? Answer- you can't.

But you can study the phenomena and try to explain them scientifically.

It would be nice to think we are not alone in the universe. It is tempting to believe in UFOs but is that realistic or wishful thinking?

SUMMARY

We can't provide the volcanos or the clear skies, but the hobbies chosen can all be adapted to your own homes. Music is so varied in Chile that you can find almost any style to suit you. Collecting stories and images of flags can be strangely compelling, but if you need a break, the Chilean desserts will boost your energy levels, if only temporarily.

Poetry, like music, can be a very personal hobby. Finding the right words and rhythm can be daunting, yet writing poetry can be done anywhere. It's just a matter of finding a style that suits you. Finally, UFO spotting is a grand sport. After all, are we alone in the universe?

Chilean Music
Flags and their Stories
Chilean Ice Cream (and Other Desserts)
Poetry Composing
UFO Hunting

CROATIA

Croatia - a land with a thousand islands – is beautiful, friendly, and a place where people love sports of all kinds, including soccer, volleyball, basketball, handball, and water polo.

The country is predominantly Roman Catholic, so Catholic traditions and ceremonies are important in everyday life. Incredible medieval architecture survives in the City of Dubrovnik, which is very photogenic, with the Bokar fortress perched high above the Pile Gate, stern protection for the area. Dubrovnik is known as the 'Pearl of the Adriatic.'

I have picked out four hobbies inspired by Croatia that you might enjoy.

CHRISTMAS MARKETS

Zagreb, the capital of Croatia, has been named the top Christmas market in Europe for three years in a row. And it runs for about six weeks.

Browsing amongst the stalls, mulled wine in hand amidst the cheerful crowds, will take you back to childhood. With snowflakes falling lazily and carols singing, you get a sense of the magic and love that Christmas is supposed to be about.

As adults, we probably prefer the giving to the receiving of gifts? But we also know our bank and credit card statements lurk in the background. How much better if we can prepare a little each month so that we are ready when Christmas suddenly steals upon us unexpectedly, despite the calendar. Our presents only need wrapping, our cards only need signing, and the Christmas cake needs a last tot of rum.

If there are Christmas markets near where you live, everything you can possibly want is there for the buying. But, last-minute shopping can be expensive, and you might not find the perfect gift you are looking for. But you can always buy ahead, ready for next year.

Many people like presents that show thought and originality, so making your own gifts most likely will be appreciated; a home-knitted scarf is more valuable than the most expensive shop-bought one, and a piece of jewelry, carefully crafted by you, is a gift to treasure. And homemade cards can show off your skills and be designed especially for the recipient.

So, go to the markets for inspiration, buy what you can afford and love, but spend time making your own gifts during the year. Many hobbies in this book lend themselves to that.

PUPPETRY

In 1919, the first Croatian puppet play was performed, called the 'Clever Donkey.' Then, after WWII, Croatia created a network of professional puppet theaters. Glove puppets and rod puppets were added to the original marionettes. At first, traditional themes predominated, a retelling of well-known fairy tales, but then a more modern style was introduced. The puppets became more symbolic and less realistic to look at.

By the 1970s, puppets were seen as a form of visual poetry, music, and mime. Puppet festivals, teaching, and courses in the art of puppetry have emerged. The Department of Theater History keeps details of puppet drama, sketches, press clippings, photographs, and texts.

Making puppets can be as simple as tiny finger puppets (which could fit into homemade crackers) to the elaborate marionettes the professional puppet masters use. Once you start, it is easy to become engrossed in puppet making as a hobby.

WATER POLO OR SWIMMING

Some say that you are never too old to start playing water polo. The rules of the game can be adapted for older players or those with disabilities.

Yet water polo has been assessed as the most strenuous summer Olympic game, based on strength, endurance, speed, and agility. And Croatians are very good at it, gaining popularity amongst the younger generations.

While water polo is excellent for building self-esteem and socializing, you might find you enjoy a less strenuous activity like swimming which is great for all ages.

Swimming burns calories, improves circulation, lowers blood pressure, and reduces your risk of heart attacks. It uses all your muscle groups to get a good workout. It's also a low-impact sport, so swimming can be an excellent way to keep fit without the risk of injury or strain on joints. Why not check for pools in your area and find suitable times when they are not too crowded, so you can take your time and enjoy a good swim.

CROATIAN PALAČINKE CREPES

There are many kinds of pancakes and many types of crepes. Palačinke is a mixture of the two without needing a leavening agent. They originated in Roman times and have remained popular ever since. Cooking can be a rewarding hobby, especially when you become known for that one special food.

The batter is thicker than crepe batter but thinner than pancake batter – and the results are mouth-watering. It will keep for up to three days in the fridge. The crepes can be stuffed with savory or sweet fillings, prepared in advance, and even frozen between sheets of waxed or parchment paper.

Kept in an airtight container, you can take out as many as you want and reclose the container (although it will be tempting to remove them all.) Then pop them in a pan or the microwave for a tasty treat.

Street vendors sell them, families have their own special fillings, and they can be a meal in themselves. Moreover, they are quick to prepare; here is one well-tested recipe that makes about ten crepes:

Ingredients

3 large eggs
1 cup milk
1/2 cup club soda – this makes them light and airy
1 cup all-purpose flour
1/2 teaspoon fine salt
1 1/2 to 2 tablespoons butter, divided
1 1/2 to 2 tablespoons avocado or grapeseed oil

Method

- Whisk the eggs and milk together and mix in the club soda.
- Add the flour and salt and whisk to remove most of the lumps. This is the tricky bit – cover and let it rest for half an hour at room temperature.
- Cook in a skillet in thin layers, using a mix of oil and butter.
- Brown each side and turn it out onto a plate.

- Stack them until all are cooked – serve and enjoy.

PHOTOGRAPHY

Croatia has them all if you like stunning views, interesting snapshots of life, and ancient urban landscapes. You can find a vast library of beautiful photographs featuring Croatia, and it's worth trawling through some of these for a pleasant afternoon's occupation when it's raining outside, and the fire is cozy and warm.

Much of 'The Game of Thrones' was photographed in Croatia, making excellent entertainment for a winter evening if you like that kind of thing.

But anyone can take photographs. They not only provide a commentary on your life and interests, but they can also produce some artistic items to display. Better still, digital photography has many ways to correct mistakes, emphasize the good points, change the colors and proportions, and make a simple photograph a work of art.

All you need is a digital camera to start producing some fine images. Later more expensive equipment might be required, but photography offers an enormous range of opportunities. You can find many programs on the internet, from simple ones like Canva to more complex programs, so why not give it a go and create some fantastic photographs.

SUMMARY

Croatia is a land that welcomes you. The people are hospitable, and the place can give you a nostalgic sense of childhood. There is magic in the air.

Christmas Markets
Puppetry
Water Polo or Swimming
Croatian Palačinke Crepes
Photography

ICELAND

Iceland is beautiful, and despite a somewhat harsh climate, Icelanders have some of the longest lifespans in the world. But the population is small, around 320,000 people. Counting all the people who have lived here since the Vikings settled in the 9th century, the number comes to less than one million. But if you count the tourists who visited in just one year, the number approaches double that.

Iceland is a land of contrasts, hot thermal springs and glaciers, volcanoes and cold seas, and for some, a tongue-in-cheek belief in elves. They have some delightful customs – Husband's Day and Wife's day, Bun Day and Beer Day, and Sjómannadagur – a day devoted to the Seamen of Iceland. They also have a 'Party Weekend' or 'Merchant's Weekend' at the start of August.

Per capita, people believe Iceland has the most beautiful women in the world, the strongest men, the most Nobel Prize winners, the best baseball team, and so on. In addition, Iceland is often top of the list for the most naturally beautiful country, the most LGBTQ friendly, the most gender-equal, and the cleanest country.

There are some seemingly odd customs, though. At various times, beer was banned, dogs were banned, and whistling or singing outside was banned.

Their hobbies reflect their Viking inheritance, so let's see what I've chosen.

GENEALOGY

There are only about 320,000 people who call Iceland home. They are nearly all descended from a small group of Vikings, but the interesting part is that the DNA shows that while the men are largely Viking, the women have the DNA of Celtic ancestors. What this means is open to interpretation, but did the Viking raiders seize the women from mainland Scotland and carry them off to their lair in Iceland?

Genealogy matters – you do not want to inadvertently engage with a close relative. Some students developed an app with the tagline, "Bump in the app before you bump in bed." There is also a highly popular website that offers access to Icelandic family trees.

Have you looked into your own ancestry? Church records, deaths, and wills can be fruitful sources of interest. Making your own family tree may lead you down some interesting pathways. My English friend, for example, told me how her ancestor was hanged in the market square, and yet she has now become the mayor of that same town.

Your children and grandchildren might find the stories you discover fascinating.

PATTERNS IN KNITTING

Icelandic knitted garments are highly valued for their high quality and intricate patterns.

The Icelandic wool has been cultivated over generations to stand up to the elements in a climate that can be cold and wet. The original settlers brought their sheep from Norway in the 9th century AD, and the breed has remained purebred and not mixed with other sheep.

The sheep's coats are well adapted to harsh weather conditions. The outer layer is long and coarse – known as 'tog.' This layer is tough and water-resistant. The inner layer is softer and keeps the sheep warm even if some water evades the tog layer and seeps down into the 'pel,' or inner layer.

When these two layers are incorporated into Icelandic knitted garments, the human inside keeps warm even in the snow and rain.

When humans knitted the clothes, the tog and pel were separated, but with the advent of industrial knitting machines, that is no longer possible. 'Lopi' is the name given to the dual wool of Iceland, and the resulting garments are wonderfully warm in cold, icy weather.

The sheep have a range of colors in their coats – black, white, various browns, or grey. Traditional knitting patterns using the natural colors are a feature of Icelandic knitting, and one is said to be able to tell which family knitted a particular sweater by the pattern. These patterns are handed down through the generations and are unique to the family concerned. And knitting is not just for women – men have been knitting for hundreds of years.

Infants were said to learn to knit as soon as they could crawl! And the results were an important economic export. So knitting was never just for granny.

You can find Icelandic patterns to try out yourself and buy the expensive-but worth-the-price Lopi Icelandic wools. Knitting and producing something special is a satisfying way to engage the hands while listening to music or watching television. Why not set up a group knitting club?

FERMENTED SHARK

If you are brave and like to taste exotic foods – why not try Hákarl or fermented shark?

Icelanders can trace this back to the Viking era; they feel it is one way to keep in touch with their ancestral past. In those far-off days, the people needed to find food to last out the long winters, and sharks were plentiful.

But there was a snag. Shark meat is poisonous. The shark's meat contains high levels of trimethylamine oxide and uric acid. This mixture helps stop the shark from freezing in the icy arctic waters but is lethal to humans.

So, the Vikings had to find a way to make sharks' meat safe to eat and long-lasting. This is how they did and still do it.

First, the shark is beheaded and gutted. Then it is put in a shallow hole dug in the sand and covered with gravel and sand. Next, the mound is pressed with large stones, squeezing the fluids out.

The shark is left to dry out for a few weeks and then cured by chopping it up into pieces and hung out to dry further. This can take a few months. The strips of shark meat develop a crust – which is removed before eating.

People say it smells like very strong cheese, but if you can get past the strong ammonia smell, the fish is edible. Some people think of this as a delicacy and are prepared to pay high prices.

Visitors to Iceland can join a local food tour and experience the Hákarl firsthand. So, here's the challenge, can you stomach Hákarl? Or can your friends stomach Hákarl? Not really a hobby, but what if you got into delicacies from around the world? Learning, studying, experiencing, and sharing these foods?

SAUCES IN ICELAND

Icelanders love their sauces. And what a variety they have.

You might think a hot dog should have ketchup, mustard, and onions? Well, in Iceland, they have a special hotdog mustard called Pylsusinnep, which differs from other mustards. They also add ketchup and 'remuladi' (remoulade). This sauce is based on mayonnaise and is rarely used except on hotdogs. It is said that Pylsusinnep will be used "every day from now until the sun swallows the Earth." It's that important for the Icelandic hotdog.

But many other sauces are used, especially béarnaise sauce, gravy, mushroom sauces, and brown sauces. In fact, any sauce you can think of is quite likely to be part of Icelandic cuisine. They have a unique sauce for fish, meat, pizza, chips, and anything else. There are sweet sauces too, like caramel, chocolate, licorice, and many more for fruits and desserts.

Perhaps you have not been a big fan of sauces, but maybe you are missing something? There are many recipe books devoted simply to sauces, so if you enjoy your hand in cooking, why not study sauces and try some out? Could you even get inspired to create your own secret sauce?

TINY HORSES

Horseback riding in Iceland is rather special. Over 1,000 years ago, the Vikings brought their shaggy little horses to Iceland, and their breed has remained genetically the same ever since.

Breeding with other stock made the very qualities that enabled the Icelandic horses to flourish in the harsh climate decline. Because of this, the Icelandic Althing (their Parliament) banned importing horses to Iceland in 928 AD. So, they have been protected for over 1,000 years!

The Icelandic sagas and legends tell of horses. In the 12th century, according to the 'Book of Settlements,' a certain man owned a horse named Skalm. He let Skalm choose where her settlement should be. When she stopped walking and lay down, that was where her settlement was founded.

Unlike most horses, who have three natural gaits (maybe four), Icelandic horses have five natural gaits. Walk, trot, and gallop are usual, but add to these the Tolt and the Flying pace. The Tolt is smooth and fast. One foot is always in contact with the ground. You can hold a glass of beer while riding and drink the full glass at the end of a Tolt. The Flying pace is fast. Both legs on one side of the horse touch the ground at the same time.

Every two years, the National Icelandic Horse Competition is held, and people come from all over the world, but like several other things, betting is banned in Iceland.

These horses are small, so the maximum weight limit for the riders is 110 kg (240 lbs).

Now you probably won't have access to an Icelandic horse, but maybe there are riding stables near you. Even if you have never ridden, horse riding is both stimulating and relaxing. Perhaps restarting childhood riding lessons might be nostalgic for you. Loving contact with animals is said to be one of the most beneficial things we can do. So why not look into the possibilities close to home?

SUMMARY

Iceland has so much to offer. With its unique customs and breathtaking scenery with active volcanoes, glaciers, and hot springs, the hobbies reflect the Viking inheritance in these tough, independent people.

Genealogy is central to their way of thinking about themselves and is even mirrored in the lovely knitting, using natural fibers from their hardy sheep and familial inherited patterns. One can't leave Iceland without tasting their foods, disgusting or highly sought after according to your sense of smell. Maybe that is why they have developed their sauces into a fine art.

The gorgeous little sturdy horses make riding seem a very attractive past-time, and the interaction between horse and man or woman can be deeply healing.

Genealogy
Patterns in Knitting
Fermented Shark
Sauces in Iceland
Tiny Horses

NEPAL

Nepal was a land of mystery until it opened up to explorers, trekkers, tourists, and serious mountaineers. Mount Everest is the highest mountain in the world, and Nepal shares its summit with Tibet (Tibetan Autonomous Region of China.)

But mountaineering is not a usual hobby for the Nepalese. Instead, it's a job that is well paid but dangerous. Since the first expedition to Mount Everest in the 1920s, at least 90 Sherpas, the high-altitude guides and porters, have lost their lives on the mountain.

Nepal is also home to the famous elite soldiers, the Gurkhas, with their signature knives, the Khukhris. But Nepal is a haven of peace and tolerance, with a strong religious presence and traditional cultures alongside the imported western cultures and strong ties with Tibet.

Hobbies are often associated with religion, such as the making and turning prayer wheels, musical instruments, and dance masks. Now they make many of these for the tourist trade. Silver jewelry, often inlaid with turquoise, metal statues, and bells, are just a few of the crafts undertaken in Nepal. They also make unique paper from the inner bark of the Lokta plant, which is exceptionally durable, tough, and resistant to insects and mildew.

Let's look at four hobbies you might be able to adapt for yourself.

PICNICS NEPAL STYLE

Picnics are one of the most popular activities in Nepal. Stunning scenery and company you like contribute to the occasion. But what is perhaps different is the way the Nepalese organize the picnic.

They are seen as social gatherings where each guest brings a contribution to the feast. One just hopes that not everyone brings a salad! Part of the pleasure is in the variety and perhaps unexpectedness of the offerings.

In Nepal, the typical type of picnic is on a table in someone's backyard, but it's outside, and hopefully, the sun will shine. Other times the family will take a drive or maybe meet up with friends, and Nepal has so many lovely places to visit.

There are even official picnics, a time for staff to bond. Simple sports, singing, and dancing may take place. For others, it's just a time to relax in good company, and eating and drinking are pleasurable activities.

I expect there are some pretty places near where you live? So, drive out into the country with family and friends to picnic. It is a great way to spend an afternoon (or a day), especially if you do not have to prepare all of the food yourself.

ACRYLIC FLUID MOUNTAIN ART

Nepal is a country of mountains, so it is no surprise to find their art reflects this.

Acrylic fluid art is a form of painting that uses acrylic paint that is more fluid than traditional acrylics. The color pigments are the same, but the effects can be lovely, and mountains make fantastic subjects. Might you like to try fluid art?

In Nepal, you don't have to go far to see incredible vistas, but there is no reason why you can't make up your own mountains, seas, forests, or even abstract color and texture artworks.

You can buy fluid art supplies or make your own from acrylic paints, acrylic mediums, and water. Canvas makes a good base, but a wooden board is even better for longer-lasting works. You will need to prepare the surface and seal the finished item to make it waterproof.

If you need inspiration, check out Nepalese flow art, which you can find in a video or on the internet. You may not be able to produce a masterpiece on your first efforts, but the technique is easy to learn and the results magnificent. You may decide to introduce silicone which disrupts the flow and makes for a marbling effect.

There are beginner sets enabling anyone to produce stunning pieces of artwork, and it's great fun. You might even start a group in your kitchen or yard.

FELTING

For many centuries, felting has been a traditional occupation in the remote villages of Nepal. The material created is tough and warm, ideal for rugs to insulate their homes from the extreme cold.

Maybe you have accidentally felted a lovely woolen sweater and then thrown it away? It's so easy to do. But felting, appropriately done, lends itself to many creative arts. You can make hats, rugs, toys, shawls, and useful or decorative things.

Felting is possibly one of the oldest arts in Nepal. Practical and using available resources. In Nepal, it's usually sheep's wool from their tough, hairy animals. But this is a craft you can do at home. Since tourism is one of Nepal's most important economic trades, many felt items are made specifically for the tourist industry.

What does felting do?

The woolen fibers are compressed and bonded together to create a dense fabric. This can be thick, thin, shaped, and long-lasting. Many mammalian fibers mat together when wet, so moisture, heat, and movement are used to make felt. This can be done by hand, but your washing machine can save time and energy.

You need to look up the instructions for making felt if interested. You might like to buy a starter kit at first, but as you get experienced, you will want to branch out, experimenting and producing some unique and versatile felts.

This hobby is not very expensive and is not very difficult until you advance to intricate designs and tiny details. If you need inspiration, look at images of the articles for sale in Nepal.

As Oscar Wilde said, "The mark of all good art is not that the thing done is done exactly or finely, for machinery may do as much, but that it is worked out with the head and the workman's heart."

SINGING BOWLS

Controversy surrounds the origin of the singing bowls. Did they originate in Tibet, or do they have a Nepalese origin?

Indeed, when Tibetan refugees fled to Nepal, some brought their singing bowls with them. As a result, whatever the origin, singing bowls can be found all over Nepal.

The bowls may be handmade, although now many are made by machine for the tourists. They can be plain or engraved, and the older bowls were usually made from a copper/tin mix, a kind of brass called 'bell metal.' Other trace metals can be added. The 'bell metal' is hard yet elastic enough to vibrate well when struck. When you rub a small wooden stick on their rim, they 'sing,' a soft, mellow sound said to have healing powers.

In Nepal, many healers use meditation and singing bowls, which create an aura like a shield to protect your body from the world's negative energy. Yet these bowls have been used for hundreds of years by Buddhas as alms bowls. But, perhaps as a marketing tool, the 'singing' bit wasn't added until the 1960s.

If you own one of these beautiful bowls, then you are fortunate. If not, technology has come up with apps you can try that have healing frequencies. Some have been devised to help you get to sleep, and some have been devised with specific frequencies to target areas of your body that may be troubling you.

Indeed, music can change our moods, and music therapy has been successfully used for people with autism and those suffering from Alzheimer's disease, dementia, and strokes. Maybe you could try meditation with some gentle music to enhance the experience. Try out several bowls or apps to find ones that resonate with you.

SUMMARY

Nepal has so much to offer, but I wanted to find hobbies that you could do yourself, and climbing Everest might not be practical for most of us. However, trekking adventures in Nepal might well be something you would like to do, but I saved that for when you visit the country.

I liked the idea of a picnic when everyone contributes the food, a friendly and entertaining social occasion. Acrylic fluid mountain art appears fun and not too difficult to get started.

Felting leads to many possibilities; maybe that old sweater could be felted and turned into adorable slippers? Finally, why not try the gentle sound of the singing bowls to relax you.

Picnic Nepal Style
Acrylic Fluid Mountain Art
Felting
Singing bowls

JAMAICA

What do you think of when you think about the Caribbean? Pirates, coffee, rum, and reggae, maybe? But there are some surprises as well.

Jamaica is home to some beautiful waterfalls, gorgeous beaches, and a rich history that is now a part of the landscape. There are over 1,600 churches in the 4,244 square miles of Jamaica, the densest church population anywhere, and the Christian religion is paramount, public prayers commonplace.

Electricity came here before it came to New York and Ian Fleming wrote his 14 James Bond books here. 'Dr. No' and 'Live and Let Die' were also filmed here. The world's fastest sprinter, Usain Bolt, comes from Jamaica, like many other world-class athletes.

I have chosen four hobbies to give you a taste of this remarkable island.

PIRATES AND THEIR HISTORY

Once upon a time, Port Royal was a 'pirate utopia.' Back in the early 1600s, Port Royal was one of the most dangerous cities in the world and acted as a base for some well-known pirates, including the legendary Welshman Henry Morgan. It was ideally situated for pouncing on merchant ships since the trade routes were very close by.

The legends about Morgan are numerous but include the facts that he raided Spanish settlements and shipping, becoming a wealthy plantation owner. In addition, it's said he dabbled in alchemy and found the secret to eternal life. Yet as he died, he gave his 'magic' compass to one 'Jack Sparrow!' And the character of Jack Sparrow may or may not be based on a real pirate, the best known of all the Caribbean pirates, the infamous Blackbeard.

But what can you do as a pirate hobby? Their history is confusing, and unraveling it might be quite fascinating. Who were they? Where did they hang out? Who paid them (the English government?)

Drawing maps, learning about the trade routes, and revisiting some of their hideouts could keep one busy for many happy hours. If you have grandchildren, why not make a booklet for them, all about real pirates?

GOLF

You might be surprised at this choice of hobby, but Jamaica has some rather unique golf courses.

Some are challenging, some more relaxing, but golf is a game that suits the sweeping landscapes of Jamaica. Taking in the shorelines and the mountains, with harmonious views and historical monuments, the courses are varied and suit any handicap.

Jamaica has been building up a reputation for golf over the past few years, with names like 'The White Witch Club' and 'The Half Moon Club.'

Golf is a popular game the world over, and it is one you can join at any age, enjoying time outside. Golf is also a chance for private conversations and bonding with friends. The competitive element need not get in the way of a good workout, fresh air, and that well-earned drink afterward.

JERK SAUCE AND ACKEE & SALTFISH

Jamaicans love spicy food, and jerk sauce is spicy! So they add it to everything like fish, chicken, or meat, giving a rather unique taste to sometimes a bland dish.

Fortunately, you do not have to make it from scratch since you can buy original jerk sauce anywhere and purchase different recipes according to your taste and the type of food. Fish and meat may require specific spices to liven them up.

Most countries have a 'national dish,' and Jamaica has 'Ackee and Saltfish.' Ackee is a fruit of the genus Blighia. Why named thus?

In 1793, Captain Bligh, of 'Mutiny on the Bounty' fame, transported ackee from Jamaica to Kew Gardens, England. Sometimes it is called the ackee apple, native to tropical West Africa. But you have to take care since unripe fruit can cause a vomiting sickness and even kill you. You must avoid the black seeds at all costs. Wait till the fruit opens naturally and the outer pods are red. But the yellow flesh is delicious.

The salt fish is just codfish that has been salted. Together with the jerk sauce, they make a tasty and spicy dish. In fact, National Geographic ranked it as the second-best national dish globally, directly under the United States hamburger.

So why not have a Caribbean evening, add some reggae music, buy some jerk sauce and prepare Ackee and Saltfish for your guests. You are almost sure to want to repeat the experience.

REGGAE

Jamaican music includes mento, dancehall, rocksteady, dub music, and ska, but the most well-known is reggae. Reggae is based on ska and early Jamaican music featuring drums, bass guitar, electric guitar, and a scraper. The scraper is a corrugated stick that you rub with a plain stick to make a unique scraping sound. The heavy four-beat rhythm is characteristic.

Then came Bob Marley, and a legend was born. With his backing band, The Wailers, he hit the international scene with such songs as "Little Birds," "One Love," and "Redemption Song."

Reggae has become associated with the voice of the oppressed and is closely related to the Rastafarian movement. The songs are a powerful voice for empowerment.

Worldwide, people can empathize with the emotions and traditions associated with reggae. It's also a way of expressing political views – and maybe appears more truthful than some politicians' speeches.

Following the words and moving to the rhythm can be quite moving as the music speaks to our inner spirit, and reggae is no exception. Tuning into reggae can bring a taste of the Caribbean into your living room, and hearing the words can be thought-provoking. Luckily there is plenty about, such as CDs, the internet, and live concerts.

SUMMARY

Jamaica has a relaxed and pleasant land, great food, top athletes, and sometimes turbulent history.

Pirates are indelibly linked to the Caribbean, but golf seems surprising. You will love jerk sauce and ackee & saltfish, the national dish if you like spicy food. Music is a part of life here, and reggae is now a global voice for the disadvantaged and pleasant to listen to.

Pirates
Golf
Jerk Sauce and Ackee & Saltfish
Reggae

ESTONIA

Estonia has a combination of medieval history together with the most modern technology. It is a land with over 1,500 islands, lakes, and forests with a landscape sprinkled with hilltop fortresses and castles.

Tallinn, the capital, has a well-preserved medieval center, and although you can find many churches, Estonia is one of the least religious countries.

Estonia regained independence from Russia in 1991, and she joined the European Union in 2004.

Family life and oral traditions are key features in the life of Estonians; they look after their elderly. Cultural activities are popular, and nightlife and lazing on the white sandy beaches contrast with hiking and skiing. Estonia is a land of contrasts, medieval and modern, traditional and forward-looking. Here are some of the hobbies practiced in Estonia.

SINGING

"Without singing, there would be no Estonia."

Peeter Perens, conductor and artistic director of the 2019 Song Festival, said these words.

For many years, Estonia's beautiful language was the language of the peasants, but in 1869, Johann Voldemar Jannsen organized the first Song Festival. A feeling of nationalism arose – "We can be a Nation."

Songs were one activity where Estonians could feel like Estonians, although during the Russian occupation, these songs were forbidden. Large groups came together under the guise of singing, defying Moscow in singing for independence.

In June 1988, 100,000 Estonians gathered for five nights to sing protest songs until daybreak. There was a feeling of their language, their nation, their song. "The Singing Revolution" (1986-1991) culminated in 1988 when a huge song festival attended by 300,000 Estonians in Tallin, 40% of the population, made their desire for independence very clear. The Estonian flag was raised, Russian tanks were faced down, and Gorbachev gave them independence.

The songs in Estonia have two origins, the ancient Finno-Ugric culture and the German-Swiss culture. And everybody likes to sing.

Song festivals and choirs are especially popular in Estonia, and they have not only hosted it but they have also won the Eurovision song contest.

You can sing anywhere: in the shower, on the balcony, or join a choir and sing along with other like-minded people. Songs may celebrate new events or tell tales from long ago. Awakening a sense of belonging, stone age mothers probably sang to their babies, just as fathers croon to their young ones.

Singing is one of the best ways to relax the muscles of your face, where we often hold tension. So, open your mouth and let the music flow.

MEDIEVAL TOWNS

You may feel you have stepped back in time when you visit Estonia. The capital city, Tallinn, can trace its origins back to 1154. The 'Toompea,' the hill in the center, has medieval houses and winding cobbled streets. You can see the outlines of the old city wall surrounding the central area and explore the guard towers that remain today.

The old town was built in the 15-17th centuries, and exploring it on foot is a great way to enjoy the old town. If you get weary, there are green parks where you can relax. Students' cultural tours will include stories about the history of Tallinn through the ages. (And the tours are free.)

Tallinn also has an abundance of cafes where you can watch the world go by, a zoo, modern shops, a beautiful 19th-century Russian Orthodox church, and a cathedral that dates back as far as 1229.

You may not have such an ancient city to explore close to you, but everywhere has a history. Some places employ knowledgeable guides and oversee tours in places of local interest. Often these are people who have retired and have the time to learn about and then talk about the places. Maybe you would like to do this, or perhaps just root around yourself?

MUSEUM VISITS

Visiting museums is a well-liked pastime in Estonia. In 2018 there were 3.4 million visits, averaging about 2 per person. However, this is still less than the previous year.

Museums of art were the most visited, especially the Estonian Art Museum. The Kumu Art Museum is the main Art Museum. The central part is based in an attractive modern building and displays Soviet pop art and contemporary art and provides an overview of Estonian art.

The Kadriorg Art Museum is based in a baroque castle built for the Russian Tsar Peter and shows early Russian and European art. Educational programs and exhibitions help to interpret the old masters. There are also over 250 sculptures created in the 18th – 20th century for people to admire.

Visiting museums can open our eyes to other cultures, to artifacts from previous ages, and when we take our time, a visit can lead to several follow-up research projects. It's odd how we often do not visit places on our doorstep. Museum visiting can be an interesting hobby, and you might even like to become involved in volunteering to show people around, as museums are often short of staff.

CROSS-COUNTRY SKIING

Estonia has some excellent cross-country skiing areas where you glide through beautiful countryside as you tone up your whole body under safe conditions.

Before taking up any sport, you should consult your physician, but cross-country skiing is not as potentially arduous as downhill or ski jumps.

Empty forests, snow gilding the trees, flattish plains for easy skiing, and well-organized ski trails make Estonia a haven for cross-country skiing. (And if you are fortunate, you might also see the northern lights since Estonia is one of the best places to observe them.)

Skiing can be kinder to your body than running but gives a superb workout. Every muscle seems to be used, circulation improves, and cheeks glow. You can escape the crowds or ski with friends. No noise except the swish of your skis, your breathing, and perhaps the laughter of your companions.

If you are a beginner, it is a good idea to tone up your body first since cross-country skiing will be demanding. If you have weak knees, you must ask your doctor first.

Beginners need flat places to start and only then gentle hills. Soon, you will be able to undertake longer journeys in lovely scenery, and when you fall, the snow will soften the bump.

Exercise releases endorphins or 'happy hormones,' so you will feel fantastic.

THE INTERNET

Estonia is possibly the most advanced country in the world regarding using the internet and similar technologies. Does this surprise you?

This is awesome. Not long ago, Estonia was a poor backwater under Russian domination. But now they have an impressive set of technological achievements.

They have E-residency, E-government, mobile parking, and fully online banking.

Most money transactions can be done online, and the population is well educated in digital technology. Children aged six are taught, and the seniors have also been included since pensions are only paid electronically. Estonia aimed to become a 'digital nation.' In 1996, they had online banking, and mobile banking started in 2000. Electronic signatures and e-signatures began in 2002, and smartphones in 2010. So, you may never need to visit your bank or use cheques or cash.

Everywhere there is free wifi, and you can complete your tax returns online with great ease. They have ID cards and digital signatures. Estonians created the first skype software.

Your computer can be your best friend if you have some knowledge of using it. It is a wonderful source of information on every subject you can think of, but there are times when most of us could happily sling it out the window!

Maybe a hobby that would appeal to you would be to learn more about computer use? There is coding design and so much more.

SUMMARY

Go back in time or become extra modern and computer savvy. Estonia offers it all. I chose singing as our first hobby since it has been very important in gaining independence for Estonia.

Going back in time in the medieval city of Tallinn offers opportunities, and visiting museums adds to the experience. Cross-country skiing is mentally and physically challenging but remember to ask your doctor.

Singing
Medieval Towns
Museum Visits
Cross-Country Skiing
The Internet

SOUTH AFRICA

South Africa is a land with much to offer. The precious Kruger National Park, with wild animals, forests and beaches, cliffs, and the famous Table Mountain overlooking the Cape of Good Hope at the southern tip of the continent of Africa.

South Africa became independent from Great Britain in 1910. Many years of apartheid followed, but now the legal system gives similar rights to all.

However, the rich and the poor might have very different hobbies - yachting and sailing, collecting fine wines, or art, are popular with the rich, whereas arts & crafts, gardening, knitting/crocheting, and baking are pastimes for others.

Sports like Nguni stick-fighting and Dambe boxing are popular, especially Capoeira, a mixture of martial arts and dance originated in Angola. However, I have picked out common hobbies you can enjoy at home and those South African people enjoy.

ONLINE COURSES

One of the most significant increases in interest in South Africa is online courses. Almost twice as many people are interested now than just a couple of years ago.

Some courses that South Africans seem to target are higher education certificates in tourism, digital marketing, and paralegal studies. They are also interested in SEO, computer courses, and sales management, among others.

As technology improves, so do the learning opportunities, and many fascinating courses are on offer. Three that took my eye were "Extinctions: Past and Present," "Understanding Clinical Research: Behind the Statistics," and "What is a mind?" all available in South Africa.

Maybe the best course to start with would be something about project management to keep your studies on track?

Online courses offer an almost endless supply of study opportunities, whether you want a certificate at the end or simply to learn about new subjects. The people of South Africa are taking advantage of these. Are you?

CROSSWORD CREATION

Crosswords have become increasingly popular in South Africa, as well as in many other

countries. In fact, in South Africa, internet searches for crosswords have increased by 88% since the pandemic that started in 2020.

South Africa has its own unique vocabulary since several languages might be spoken there, and some of these words can end up in South African crosswords. Words like:

Lekker – nice/great – we had a lekker party
Howzit? – who is it?
Yebo: yes – comes from the Zulu
Shap sharp – all's fine
Braai – BBQ
Yoh – surprise
Robot – traffic lights

Maybe you are good with words? Possibly a challenging brain workout for you? Perhaps you could make your own crosswords, especially on a subject you know something about?

To make it easier, here are a few tips:

Choose a theme and then write a long list of words about it, short and long words. Try to link some of the longer words together. This will be the center of your grid. Fit shorter words around them.

Build up your grid with blank squares, number the first letter of every word, and create the clues!

Crosswords are in demand. Newspapers feature them, books about them are on sale, and it is possible to make money by creating and selling them.

JUKSKEI

Jukskei is a sport unique to South Africa, although it is gaining popularity across the continent.

Jukskei originates from the Afrikaners' name for the wooden pin used to yoke oxen. Around 1743, transport riders traveled by wagons drawn by oxen. They used to throw the pins at a stick planted in the ground, attempting to knock it down. The game has formal rules and is supervised by the International Jukskei Federation.

Usually, this game is played with teams of two or four, and the distance to the stick is fixed. In 2017 by the South African government, Jukskei was included in the Indigenous Games Project.

One of the largest rivers in South Africa is also named the Jukskei River, which is a branch of the Crocodile River.

This game, or your interpretation, could be quite competitive, easy to set up, and suitable for a laugh. Just keep any dogs well clear unless they could be used to retrieve your 'pins.'

MALVA PUDDING

South African food is as diverse as its different peoples. Dutch, German, English, and French mix with the many local tribes, and their unique blends of culture and cuisine have evolved into very tasty dishes.

Meat is an important ingredient in many of the foods on offer, but the desserts are to die for! Here is one sweet treat you might like to try. The origin is Cape Dutch, and it's called Malva Pudding.

Ingredients for the pudding

6 1/2 ounces sugar
2 large eggs
1 tablespoon apricot jam
5 ounces all-purpose flour
1 teaspoon baking soda
1/2 teaspoon salt
1 generous tablespoon butter
1 teaspoon vinegar
1/3 cup milk

Ingredients for the sauce

3/4 cup fresh cream
3 1/2 ounces butter
3 - 5 ounces sugar
1/3 cup hot water
2 teaspoons vanilla essence

Method

- Preheat oven to 180°C (350°F). Grease a baking dish 18 x 18 x 4 ½ cm (7 x 7 x 1 1/2 inches).
- Whip the sugar and eggs until thick. Then add the jam and mix.
- Add the melted butter and vinegar.
- Pour into the greased dish and bake until brown and risen – about 30-45 minutes (You may want to adjust the heat and time according to your oven.)
- To make the sauce, melt all the ingredients together, stirring well, and be ready to pour it over the pudding as soon as it comes out of the oven.

The hard part is leaving it to stand for a while before serving to allow the sauce to seep through.

In South Africa, they often serve this with ice cream or cream. As a winter treat, this pudding will warm the cockles of your heart. Baking can be a gratifying hobby, and I think your family and friends will agree.

CROCHETING

During the Irish potato famine, crochet came into being. It provided an income that was desperately needed.

Crochet is satisfying and quick. It's faster than knitting once you know how to do it. And it is so satisfying to create something you made yourself. In South Africa, crocheting has also provided an income for some of the poorest women, who may not have time for more demanding hobbies.

Workshops have sprung up where people can meet up, socialize, and enjoy crafting a practical, durable, and attractive item.

There are only five basic stitches, with many ways to use them, from simple squares to make shawls and blankets to delicate filigree shawls and Christening robes. This hobby is easily carried from one place to another and can be done while watching television or the children.

As a new starter, many YouTube videos can take you through the stitches step by step and show you how to read patterns. Just be sure you know whether you use European or American names for the stitches since there are differences.

If you are interested in selling your items, why not showcase them on Facebook, Etsy, or Pinterest?

SUMMARY

South Africans enjoy various unusual games and hobbies, like Nguni stick wrestling or cheetah walking, which would not be easy for us to copy. Still, they also have some very familiar things we can do at home.

More and more variety in online courses and the ease of access make these a viable proposition for most of us. Crossword creation is another way to stimulate the brain. If you want something more active, try your own version of Jukskei or to relax, settle down to create something practical with your crochet hook.

Online Courses
Crossword Creation
Jukskei
Crocheting

SAMOA

Fa'a Samoa means the Samoan Way. This has meaning to Samoans and influences the everyday lives of the Samoan people. Fa'amatai is a social system where family and village elders are expected to put the community's interests above their own interests.

This in-built service to others continues to this day, and if you visit Samoa, you will be welcomed with warm smiles, hospitality, and respect. In Samoa, the elderly are respected, and their opinions are sought. Their long experience in life is valued. Likewise, children are brought up to pay attention to their elders and obey their parents until they marry.

Many of the activities undertaken by the Samoan people are geared toward family and community bonding. Outdoor activities like surfing, diving, sea-kayaking, and island excursions are popular. They also enjoy uma cuisine, traditional crafts, cake decoration, and a DIY form of cricket called kilikiti. And for a day out, there is always the Robert Louis Stevenson Museum to visit since he used to live and write in Samoa.

SAMOAN UMU COOKING

In a typical Samoan village, the umu is a common way of cooking, and very little is needed in terms of equipment. This is not fast food, but one umu can feed many hungry people. It is an integral part of the Samoan way of life.

The umu is an oven made above the ground but uses hot volcanic stones to provide heat. Traditionally the earth oven is placed on a 'fale,' a unique stand for the umu.

Typically, the umu cooking method is handled by men, just as BBQ often is in western cultures. But anyone can use the umu cooking method.

The volcanic stones are heated up in a fire. All this takes time, so the cook might have to get up early. Volcanic rocks are good because they retain heat well. The fire is ready when the wood and coconut husks are burnt to cinders.

You first must prepare the food to load into the umu. Food may contain meat, fish, or octopus, often combined with coconut cream. Vegetables and fruit such as taro, ulu (breadfruit), and unripe bananas may be added, plus the favorite, palusami (coconut milk) with onions.

The food might be wrapped in coconut fronds, banana leaves, or coconut halves. Then the food is placed on top of the hot stones, with some stones placed gently on top. More banana leaves are settled on top to seal in the heat, so you have to wait!

Usually, the food takes around 90 minutes to bake, giving off a tantalizing, smokey yet savory, and sweet smell with a hint of coconut. Samoans have been smelling this aroma for over 300 years. The umu can be used for large families or small gatherings and is an easy way to cater to a larger group of people.

The Samoan umu is like the western BBQ, with its distinctive flavors and foods. You might try a version of the umu in your own backyard.

'IE TŌGA

The Samoan embroidered mat isn't a mat at all, even though we call them 'fine mats' in English. Made roughly the size of a bed cover, they are far too valuable to tread on.

Myths surround the origin of these fine mats. One story tells the tale of the goddess Nāfanua. She planted the first pandanus from which these mats are made at Falealupo. Near the entrance to Pulotu – the Samoan equivalent of Hades – this lies in the sea where the setting sun lights up a golden pathway.

The pandanus has a fan of long, narrow leaves and aerial, woody roots. There are two sub-species of pandanus used for mat making, the very fine one and the other a little coarser. Both types of pandanus are now grown in the villages: the more delicate the weave, the more valuable the mat.

In the past, the 'ie tōga was used as currency, but now it is used in special occasions such as processions, funerals, weddings, and the blessing of a new house or church. 'Ie tōga might be worn on special occasions, like the lavalava tied around the waist. The women make these mats, often as a communal activity, and some of the finest mats can take months to finish. The resulting shine and softness add to the value.

But what makes these 'ie tōgas so special?

Not only are they finely woven, but they are also embroidered with images and designs in colored threads and materials. They sport a fringe and a strip of red feathers (now often dyed chicken feathers.) They make valuable gifts and may be passed down to the family as heirlooms. In the past, they represented family wealth.

Now you may not have pandanus growing in your yard – and you might not want to spend months making a bedspread-sized 'mat,' but the idea of an embroidered mat is versatile.

One suggestion is to weave a mat from linen strips and then embroider it in any way you wish, appliqué and colored yarns could make your mat unique, and a small mat would make an interesting table mat for special occasions or be given away as gifts. You could even match it with table-napkin embroidered rings.

You could find plenty of images of Samoan 'ie tōgas for inspiration on the internet.

SAMOAN CAKE DECORATING

Samoa cake decorating is an art. You can see some truly unique creations from Samoa on Pinterest. Samoans thrive in cake decorating, and skills are often passed down between generations.

One example I saw was the 'Grandpa Cake.' It costs $355.00 or 6 weekly interest-free payments of $59.16, but it has a five-star rating and several flavor options. It looks far too good to eat!

There are options for cake decorating courses run in Samoa or online. You might never achieve the star quality you can see on the cakes created in Samoa, but it is an exciting hobby for the creative person.

Most everyone likes some sort of cake, and the nicer looking it is, the better. Birthdays, Christmas, and other festive days often have cake at the heart of the celebration. But not everyone has the time or the talent to create beautiful cakes. If this is something you aspire to, online or in-person instruction would be very helpful. The best thing about this hobby is that your mistakes can be eaten, and no one needs to know.

KILIKITI

English missionaries brought the game of cricket to Samoa in the early 19th century. The game is now the national sport of

Samoa, but with Samoan alterations. And kilikiti is widespread around the Pacific Ocean (but not in England.)

Players in this form of cricket wear no protective shields or padding. Their traditional lavalava sufficed. This is a wraparound skirt made from a single piece of cloth. But the ball is very hard. It is made from a hard rubber wrapped in processed pandanus leaves.

The bat is modeled on the three-sided traditional Samoan war club. It is made from wood and wrapped in sennit. Each player can have his bat, differing in length and surface angle, so it can be almost impossible to work out where the ball will be headed.

Just as bats are unique, so to are the rules flexible. In fact, only the players may know what the rules are for any given game.

However, there are some ways in which kilikiti resembles English cricket. They have fielding and batting teams and a pitch. They alternate bowlers from one end of the pitch to the other, with two wickets. The teams can be any size, and visitors are often welcomed in.

Kilikiti is very much a communal event. Everyone takes part or watches, and the kilikiti matches are fought as enthusiastically as any English cricket game.

Because you can make up your own rules, you might try a game of kilikiti in your backyard, but you don't have to field a very hard ball; just have some fun and light exercise.

SUMMARY

Samoan people are warm and friendly, and their code of conduct ensures that other people are cared for and respected. Their hobbies reflect this. Umu cooking is a slow process that gives ample time to chat and socialize with family, friends, and visitors. While you wait, you could always make a woven mat and decorate it. Cake decorating is brought to new artistic highs and kilikiti, which is just fun with few rules, or make them up to suit your team as you go along.

Samoan Umu cooking
'Ie Tōga (Fine Mats)
Samoan Cake decorating
Kilikiti (Samoan cricket)

LIECHTENSTEIN

The Principality of Liechtenstein is a tiny country between Switzerland and Austria. It is a financial center, previously a tax haven.

The head of state is the heir designated to the throne, Prince Alois. Just over 70% of the people are Catholics, so religious celebrations, as well as Valentine's Day and Mother's and Father's Days, are kept.

The main crafts used to be barrel making, basket weaving, and clog carving, although now sculpture, pottery, and woodcarving have taken over to a large extent. Liechtenstein is the world's leading exporter of false teeth.

Liechtenstein might be a small country, but it has some interesting hobbies.

CLOG CARVING

Carving clogs is a traditional hobby in Liechtenstein; although many of the clogs are made in Holland, then a hand-carved design is added in Liechtenstein.

Clogs are comfortable to wear, easy to slip on and off, and can make interesting decorations.

In Liechtenstein, doorways, and entrances often feature wood carvings. They may be flowers or a row of hand-carved clogs, sometimes with natural (not carved) flowers growing within them—what a change from ordinary flowerpots.

A set of stamps celebrates traditional crafts in Liechtenstein and feature a wagon wheel, a milk pail, and a clog.

Suppose you would like to carve something unique and not too tricky; videos on the internet explain how to go about it. First, you need to buy the plain clogs and then simply decorate them by coloring and varnishing them and then hanging them up or wearing them. After that, they are sure to be admired.

RIBEL

Ribel (or Rebl) used to be a poor man's dish in Liechtenstein. Healthy and filling, its base is cornmeal, so it's gluten-free. Now many restaurants offer Ribel, often for breakfast.

Cornmeal is a coarse flour made from maize, and maize cultivation in this area has been ongoing since at least the 16th century. Many families planted maize in their gardens. It made a perfect breakfast before a day of hard labor in the fields and was a great stand-by during the turmoil of the world wars.

To make Ribel, cook the corn, possibly with wheat, in boiling water or milk, then roast it with butter. Add apple puree for extra taste.

Here is a recipe for you to try out:

Ingredients

300 ml milk
300 ml water
1 tbsp salt
500 g Ribel corn/semolina corn
1 tbsp grapeseed oil
25 g butter

Method

- Boil the water and milk with the salt.
- Stir in the corn, and simmer over low heat. If you continuously stir it, you are less likely to create lumps. It thickens to a paste which you cover and leave for about 3 hours.
- Heat the oil in a frying pan, add the Ribel mix, and roast in the pan for about 20 minutes. Stir often and add the butter bit by bit. It will turn a golden brown.
- Enjoy with a fruit compote and coffee.

Incidentally, you don't have to get up several hours before breakfast since the mixture will keep in an airtight container in the fridge overnight.

STAMP COLLECTING

Maybe you are a stamp collector? Liechtenstein has some of the most beautiful stamps in Europe, and it is possible to find them and build up a worthwhile collection.

For Liechtenstein, they are a source of revenue for the government since the stamps can be quite valuable. Often the designs are taken from the paintings in the art collection of the Prince. Otherwise, they might depict traditional occupations, such as basket weaving and barrel making.

The stamps of Liechtenstein are associated with the stamps from Austria and Switzerland. Before 1918, Liechtenstein was part of Austria. Separate stamps for the Principality of Liechtenstein only began in 1912.

Then Switzerland took over when the Austro-Hungarian Empire collapsed after World War One. It can be expensive to collect earlier stamps, but it might be possible to build up a complete collection if one starts with stamps from 1945 onwards.

Internet auctions are one source of stamps, but you could choose another country to specialize in or simply collect pretty stamps because they look attractive. Philately, the collection and study of postage stamps, has many possibilities.

MACRO PHOTOGRAPHY

This is a slightly different slant from the popular hobby of photography. It means taking extremely close-up photos, usually of small things, insects are a common theme, and making the photograph greater than life-size. It opens up a fascinating world you could not see with the naked eye.

This differs from micro photography, where the super-close up is reproduced life-size.

Liechtenstein has photo courses to help beginners capture stunning images. There are also internet and video courses and guides available. But this is not always the easiest of hobbies to become an expert at.

You will need the right equipment, for example, a tripod and the macro-lens, and you will need to be extra careful about the lighting and focusing. However, once you have your image, you can have fun cropping it, altering brightness, sharpness, and even color.

You can find the most amazing things to photograph in your own backyard, like details of flowers, an insect's eye, or the weave of the fabric you are wearing. There is no end to possibilities. You might wish to visit a museum where such photographs might be on display, such as the Smithsonian Museum of Natural History.

SUMMARY

Liechtenstein has a mix of new and old. The recipe for Rigel is based on a nourishing peasant breakfast, but macro photography is up to date. Wood carving has always been a feature of life in Liechtenstein, and collecting stamps is a global interest, with stamps of Liechtenstein highly coveted.

Clog carving
Ribel
Stamp collecting
Macro photography

EGYPT

Egyptian history goes back a long way. The old forms of entertainment included such things as javelin throwing, swimming, chariot racing, wrestling, juggling, music, and dance. Literature was also important. Ancient Egyptians wrote poetry, puns, and spells, and in modern times Egypt has produced some of the best Arabic writers.

Many ancient ways have continued; for example, senet is still played. Music and dance continue to be important; reading, crafts, and learning about the past are enjoyable activities.

AMATEUR ARCHAEOLOGY

Amateur archaeology in Egypt is punishable with up to 25 years in prison and a fine of up to 10 million Egyptian pounds ($640,000 US dollars.) The Ministry of Antiquities vets all applications from professional archaeologists who wish to participate in excavations. They protect their past.

But when you think of Egypt, you think of the Great Pyramids and the wonders of the tombs. So many of the pharaohs resting places have been plundered. Amateur archaeologists have done so much damage to irreplaceable artifacts that it is good to know Egyptian experts are using modern technologies to make accurate recordings, preserving the past in ways unavailable until recently.

However, the study of archeology is fascinating, and several avenues are open to you. For example, you can read, study images, and watch videos in your own home.

You could also visit your local museum. They often have interesting objects on view or may be hidden away behind the scenes so ask.

But you might want to get your hands dirty and participate in an actual excavation. Many digs do welcome amateurs. You can check out suggestions here: http://www.ubarchaeologist.com, but you need to contact the team involved directly.

So, if you have ever wanted to reach back in time to physically hold something that was last touched by someone many, many years ago, in that case, Egypt might stimulate your passion, but you will have to experience the thrill of finding ancient objects elsewhere.

PAPYRUS PAPERMAKING

The Ancient Egyptians were the first people to make a paper-like material from the papyrus plant, and our English word paper is derived from this. True papermaking took place in China during the Han dynasty (25–220 CE.) But the first paper-like writing sheet was papyrus from Egypt, about 3,000 years ago.

So, what is the difference between papyrus and paper?

The Egyptians made papyrus 'paper' from natural plants. The fibers are pressed and pounded together and dried. On the other hand, paper is made from fibers that have been macerated and disintegrated.

The papyrus water plant grew in the marshy delta of the river Nile, and there was plenty of it. The outer rind is first removed to make papyrus, and thin strips are sliced off the sticky fibrous inner pith lengthwise. The strips are laid side by side, and then a second layer of papyrus strips is applied on top at right angles. Finally, the double layer is pounded together to make one strong sheet. Sometimes glue was also used.

The final sheets were polished to make the surface smoother for writing. The Egyptians used papyrus to make sails, cords, mats, and cloth. Later the Greeks and then the Romans adopted papyrus as writing material.

You can make your own 'papyrus' at home and get an authentic-looking ancient effect. If you then decorate it with Egyptian hieroglyphics, you could make some exciting and unusual items; perhaps they could be used as cards or gifts.

This is how to make your own papyrus:

1. Cover your work surfaces – it can get messy. Lay out a paper towel.
2. Have glue ready – it might be wallpaper glue that needs mixing. Strong glue is not needed.
3. Place the glue in a flattish bowl.
4. Tear a brown paper bag into strips.
5. One by one, dip the strips of paper into the glue mix and place them side by side with the edges overlapping on the paper towel.
6. Smooth the surface out.
7. Do a second layer at right angles to the first and smooth out.
8. Let it dry.
9. Your paper is ready.

HIEROGLYPHICS

Hieroglyphics are attractive to look at, and for many years they were full of mystery. Egyptian tombs are full of them.

The word is Greek, although the writing is Egyptian. The name comes from 'Hiero,' which means 'holy,' and 'glyphics,' which means 'marks.' To ancient Egyptians, there was power in a name. That is why the pharaohs had their names inscribed in their tombs. It helped them to survive in the afterlife.

A breakthrough in deciphering these strange symbols came when Napoleon's troops discovered the Rosetta stone in 1799 when they invaded Egypt. This stone has hieroglyphs and a Greek translation, although it took about 20 years to decipher completely.

You read the hieroglyphs from left to right or from right to left. The figures always point to the start of the line so you can tell which direction to read it. And you start at the top. The pictures often represent what they show, but usually, the picture stands for a sound. Sometimes the same symbol can have two meanings. For example, a mouth image can mean a mouth or the sound 'r.'

While you can often guess the meaning, the symbolism is complex and can be confusing. But it is possible to work out how to 'spell' your name.

Why not make some 'papyrus' and decorate it with hieroglyphs? Spelling out your friend's name could make a unique and thoughtful birthday card, and learning about the hieroglyphs must surely challenge the brain.

COPTIC BOOK-BINDING

The early Christians in Egypt employed a type of bookbinding called Coptic binding. This form of book-binding uses a thread to sew the layers together. A similar modern style of book-binding retains the name. But it took many years to change from storing writing in scrolls to storing it in books.

Originally the parchments were folded in half, and the sewing was done through the folded area. This made the edges uneven since the inner folded pages protruded and needed to be trimmed when the binding was done. When the book was first written, one had to determine how many pages were needed and how wide to make the margins.

Once single pages without folds were used, life became easier for the bookbinders.

The covers were usually sewn in and were often made from limp leather stiffened with papyrus, or something wooden.

Coptic binding is easy, and you can produce your own books this way. It works well for a series of sketches or a journal, and you don't need to have many pages. The internet has some good instructional videos, but it is just a matter of sewing one of the sides of the pages together with a continuous thread.

SENET

The game of senet was played as long ago as 5,000 years by the Egyptians. So popular was this game that it had been found among the funeral offerings in the graves of the dead, from pharaohs to the elite to commoners. Something to occupy them in the afterlife.

The boards could be highly decorated or simple grids – even drawings. The game is for two people; the board is marked on 30 squares in three rows of ten. Each player had between five and ten marked sticks, which they threw in turn. The aim was to progress along with the board, evading blocking movements by their opponent and getting rid of their pieces.

On the walls of the tombs of the New Kingdom, the game had taken on a religious significance, representing the path of the dead through the underworld. These boards have unique marks on the last five squares to show the arrival of eternity.

The boards were usually made from Egyptian faience, a common material used to make many small objects and ornaments. Some senet boards were made from wood. And if you are wondering what Egyptian faience is, here is a description taken from Wikipedia:

"Egyptian faience is a non-clay based ceramic composed of crushed quartz or sand, with small amounts of calcite lime and a mixture of alkalis, displaying surface vitrification due to the soda-lime-silica glaze often containing copper pigments to create a bright blue-green luster."

Since senet was so popular, it might be worth buying a board and having a few games. You could even buy several boards and start a senet playing club in your living room. Then, you might find out just why it was so popular.

SUMMARY

Egyptians have some unique interests that we can try our hand at, and the archeology of Egypt is the basis for many of these unique hobbies. Although amateur archaeologists are not welcome in Egypt, the subject can be an inspiration for hobbies such as papyrus paper making, Coptic book-binding, and learning about and writing hieroglyphics and the ancient game of senet.

Amateur Archeology
Papyrus Papermaking
Hieroglyphics – study and draw
Coptic Book-Binding
Senet

ZIMBABWE

Zimbabwe is a land of natural wonders. Victoria Falls is one of the seven natural wonders of the world, known as 'the smoke that thunders' in local languages. There are national parks full of wildlife, and the people have used the natural resources to produce some lovely craftwork. Music, dance, and song are a way of life.

They were building impressive cities of stone around 1,200 AD, including two great cities – Great Zimbabwe and Khami – and their walls survive to this day. There is a diverse population, and each ethnic group has its legends and myths and an oral recording of its stories, heroes, and past. In the daily life of Zimbabwe, the people combine the African and Western worlds. Ancestor worship continues, but about 75% also worship as Christians or Islam.

Traditional crafts and music continue to this day. Songs and stories are passed on in the rich culture of Zimbabwe. I've chosen four hobbies you could pursue in your own way.

MBIRA INSTRUMENTAL MUSIC

The Shona people of Zimbabwe have a group of traditional musical instruments called the mbira. The basic design is a wooden board with metal tines attached. The instrument is held in the hands, and the tines are plucked with thumbs and forefingers.

For thousands of years, similar musical instruments have been played in Africa. The tines were originally made from bamboo and played over 3,000 years ago. Metal tines came later, around 1,500 years ago, and became popular among the Shona people, who called them 'mbira.'

There are many forms of mbira, but 'the voice of the ancestors' is heard in the mbira dzavadzimu and plays an integral part in religious ceremonies, weddings, and social meetings. In addition, traditional music is on the UNESCO Representative List of the Intangible Cultural Heritage of Humanity.

The mbira gave rise to the kalimba, a modern, popularized version exported from Africa in the late 1950s. It might be played by bands with electric guitars, drums, and horns and incorporate many songs taken from the Shona.

The sound can be unfamiliar to western ears. There are thousands of different tunings; adjacent tines vibrate, causing secondary harmonies, and shells and bottle tops might be added to the wooden board to increase the vibratory tone. This buzzing is said to attract the spirits of the dead. The layout of the tines can be idiosyncratic, with odd notes appearing when least expected. Intervals between notes differ from Western scales.

Just as the sounds are complex, so is the rhythm. Often a 3:2 cross-rhythm, the left hand playing bass and the right hand the melody.

It is possible to buy a mbira instrument, and there are videos on the internet to teach you how to play it. It would be not only exciting and entertaining but probably extremely difficult for one brought up only on western music to acquire competence on the mbira, but what a journey.

BEADWORK

Beads have been ornamental since ancient times and in most cultures. They have been used as money for trade, to adorn the person and clothes, and to make works of art. Initially, local items such as shells, wood, and even teeth were threaded and used as status symbols and decorations.

When glass beads were manufactured in bulk, they became essential items of trade. And now we are fortunate to have a huge variety of beads with all kinds of uses. Glass beads were imported to Zimbabwe in the 7th century from places as far away as Sri Lanka and the Persian Gulf. The Portuguese brought glass beads into the country to exchange for gold dust, ivory, and tobacco.

The beadwork of the BaTonga, of Zimbabwe and Zambia, is outstanding for the variety, color, and intricacy of the designs. Zimbabwe is known for bead wall art, tree decorations, and small animal ornaments. The most commonly chosen animals are their native wild animals, making them rather unique.

They also use glass beads to define the different stages of a woman's life, perhaps as a skirt for small girls with white beads that reflect the light and seem to express the joy of childhood. Traditional healers may wear distinctive beadwork to help identify their calling. The beads may work as charms against evil spirits or bring good luck to the wearer.

The little wire and bead animals look very cute, and there are kits available, so you could build up a collection of these ornaments or make some scintillating tree decorations.

BASKETRY

Crafts are an important source of income for many families in Zimbabwe, and the beautiful baskets produced are one of the most successful traditional crafts.

This is particularly true for the Tonga women in northwest Zimbabwe. They use materials found locally, such as grass, fronds from palm trees, and reeds. 'Binga' baskets, named for the town, use a hard vine and ilala palm.

Originally, these baskets were used for winnowing grain and are still used for this purpose. However, they are used for fruit, bread, placemats, dishes, or decorating walls. The patterns can be pretty intricate and decorated with natural tree-bark dyes. A simple over-and-under-weaving technique is employed, but a 16-inch diameter basket can take up to three days to finish. Finally, the coiled rim is completed using a herringbone pattern.

The designs are inspired by nature and learned through apprenticeship within families.

The export of these baskets is a welcome source of income for village families. Indeed, it has enabled many families to send their children to school.

Basketry is available to all of us. We may not be able to source local plants, but there are many alternatives, and many educational facilities hold basket weaving courses. They are a practical and decorative addition to anyone's home.

MUBOORA UNE DOVI TRADITIONAL DISH

Muboora Une Dovi is a traditional African dish that comes from Zimbabwe. To create this delicious dish, combine pumpkin leaves, tomato, onion, salt, baking soda, peanut butter, and oil. Carefully wash your pumpkin leaves, then simmer in a pot of boiling water with salt and baking soda until fully cooked.

Ingredients (serves 3 - 4)

1 bundle muboora (young pumpkin leaves and stems)
2 cups water
1 tsp baking soda
1 tsp salt
1 Tbsp oil
1 tomato, roughly chopped
2 Tbsp smooth peanut butter
1 onion, roughly chopped

Method

- Once cooked, drain the excess water and set aside while you make the sauce.
- Heat oil in a saucepan over medium heat. Add onion and cook until softened.
- Add tomato, stir well and cover with a lid. Cook for 5 minutes, then stir in peanut butter.
- Mix well, adding enough boiling water to make a thick paste.
- Add your pumpkin leaves and combine.

Muboora is typically served with sadza (Zimbabwe staple) or rice. Why not start a monthly supper club in your community as a hobby? Each month could be a different country to focus on. What a fantastic way to learn about other cultures while enjoying delicious food.

SHONA SCULPTURES

Hanc sculpture is a relatively modern term, but the Shona people have been working with stone for hundreds of years. For example, the Great Zimbabwe Settlement was an 11th -

15th-century town built of stone and housing up to 1,800 people. This is now a world heritage site for the Shona people.

But now, the Shona sculpture means artistic stone-carved works. The name Shona comes from the mix of tribes known as Shona. The sculptures have close links with cultural and spiritual practices many still practiced today. Only relatively recently has this Zimbabwe's art achieved worldwide recognition, which is still evolving.

Millions of years ago, an extremely rich vein of Serpentine rock, stretching for hundreds of miles, was laid down and is now on the surface. Many of the stones used are members of the Serpentine family, and they have a range of colors from dark green-black to brighter but less common colors. While Springstone is the most commonly used stone, many different varieties of stone are carved to produce a range of styles and colors.

Opal Stone is another softer variant than serpentine, smooth and glossy, with specks of red and blue. With its purple or green coloring and lighter markings, Cobalt stones are brittle and apt to break, but the results can look marvelous.

Dolomite is soft and suitable for more significant works, and sometimes it is tinged with iron or has transparent white crystals, giving the finished product a pearl-like appearance.

Butter Jade might look like butter, but it is hard and long-lasting. Despite its name, it is not a true jade and is rare outside South Africa. Sapolite, lemon opal, and leopard stone are other variants the sculpture might use.

Carving stone might not be a suitable hobby for you, but collecting them could be. They would certainly make an unusual collection and could lead to social contacts in many countries.

SUMMARY

Zimbabwe is a country where people have embraced music and song to tell their history. The traditional Mbira musical instrument might take a great deal of practice to perfect playing, but listening to the different intonations can stimulate the brain. Their crafts reflect the incredible wildlife found in their natural parks, and the cute little wire and bead animals plus the wall art are things that would be possible to enjoy at home. Basketry is a hobby that can be DIY at home or as a social gathering, and collecting the Shona people of Zimbabwe's stone sculptures is a hobby growing worldwide.

Mbira instrumental music
Beadwork
Basketry
Muboora Une Dovi Traditional Dish
Shona sculptures

MEXICO

Mexico is full of color and movement, and humor. From their masks to their dances, from their art to their care for children. The people of Mexico have a rich and entertaining set of crafts and hobbies.

Like most of us, they go shopping, read and watch television. Family life is important, and children take an active part in the social life of Mexicans. So, large family meals, caravans, and camping are popular activities, and with the sunny beaches and blue sea, they have a wide choice of places to go.

I have chosen six activities you might enjoy, so let's dive in.

JARABE TAPATÍO DANCE

The Jarabe Tapatío is the national dance of Mexico. It is often known as the Mexican Hat dance in the USA, but it is far more than that and has a somewhat checkered history.

The theme of the dance is the courtship of a man with a lady he meets at a party. The dance starts by dancing around a sombrero, hence the alternative name. At first, she rejects his advances, but ultimately, she accepts them, and he may raise his hat to hide a kiss.

This dance originated in Western Mexico during the 19th century, although some elements predate this, going back to the Spanish Zambra. The music, composed by Jesus Gonzalez Rubio, and the dance represent Mexico.

Why Jarabe? This is derived from the Arabic for "mixed herbs" and reflects the mix of different Mexican dances and music. While other versions of Jarabe exist, the Tapatio version is the best known.

Originally, the Jarabe Tapatio was danced only by women to avoid religious censorship. By 1790 mixed couples performed, but soon after, the dance was banned as Spanish colonial and religious authorities thought it morally offensive. The result was that the dance became even more popular, and people held dances illegally as a form of protest.

After independence in 1861, the dance became even more popular, widely celebrated in festivals and fiestas. The dance is still taught in most Mexican schools to this day.

To learn how to do the Jarabe Tapatio, you either need to study videos, and there are several on the internet or attend classes. Dancing the Jarabe Tapatio would be enormous fun, and watching a performance would make for great entertainment.

MEXICAN YARN ART

Mexico is well known for the bright colors and artistic talent of the people. Yarn art is no exception.

Traditional Neirikas are yarn paintings that the people of Huichol make. They make their own glue from beeswax and tree resin, then paste it onto a board. First, a pattern is scratched on the surface of the wax. Then the yarn is pressed into it to make a bold, colorful pattern, filling in all the spaces; it is left to harden. The designs themselves represent local myths and tales and illustrate everyday life.

The Huichol people of Mexico live in small villages in the Sierra Madre. The gods are essential; there will be houses for the gods or even caves, and people bring gifts, such as flowers, feathers, prayer bowls, and yarn art. They hope their gifts will bring them luck.

What the gift symbolizes matters. Neirika means 'face,' and the face depicted might be the face of the wind or the face of the harvest. They might be expressing a wish; a face of water or a serpent might mean a longing for rain, and the face of the sun a wish for a good harvest.

Maybe you have a wish you could make a face for? Or maybe you just enjoy making something attractive and unusual.

You can also try making your own yarn art. You will need a stiff card for the base, white glue (PVA works well), scissors, and several colored yarns. You may find a toothpick useful for scratching your pattern, and you will probably need plenty of paper towels.

There are many uses for these yarn pictures. You can use them to decorate boxes, cover notebooks, and create cards and pictures for your wall, and they make perfect gifts.

The internet has many inspiring examples, but you may prefer to think up your own patterns to represent a much-loved pet or a swirly sea scene with colorful fish. The possibilities are endless.

WORRY DOLLS

Worry dolls originated in Guatemala but are widely popular in Mexico, and for good reason.

They are small, hand-made little dolls that one can use in several ways to relieve anxiety and worry. This is especially helpful for children.

The legend goes that a Sun god gave a Mayan princess called Ixmucane a special gift. This gift would let her resolve any problem that might worry her. The traditional way to use a worry doll was to tell the doll about your worries and then place the doll under your pillow and go to sleep. In the morning, you would wake up with all the skills and wisdom needed to solve the problem.

Modern psychology shows that, indeed, our brains do sort things out during our sleep. It's important to realize that this process does not teach us that there are no worries, but it is a tool for helping us deal with what life throws at us.

These little dolls are often homemade, from wool, wire, pressed paper, and little pieces of colorful textiles. While most dolls are tiny, under 3 inches tall, they can be made to any size to suit you. Traditionally, they are dressed in a Mayan style of clothing.

Anyone can make their own worry dolls from familiar everyday things like popsicle sticks, cloth from old clothes, sellotape, or glue. Or maybe collect stuff from a nature walk like sticks, feathers, etc. It can be a bit more exciting if you have some googly eyes for them. Making your own dolls makes it unique for you.

MEXICAN MASKS

For thousands of years, the people of Mexico have been making masks. They played their part in rituals, theater, and processions. Religious ceremonies and burials are where the wealthiest dead had masks made from precious materials such as jade and decorated with shells.

When the Spanish arrived, they adapted the masks to the Catholic faith.

The masks are still a part of the culture, especially in 'Lucha Libre,' which is a form of wrestling. The use of an animal mask was said to give the strength and cunning of the animal to the fighter. Some of these masks are handed down from father to son for several generations. But in some matches, the loser must remove his mask, which may never be worn again.

Many other popular mask themes include animals, demons, and fantasy figures. Dancing and many other uses for the masks are still around. Religions and fiestas amalgamated, and many masked dancers participated in festivals and Holy Week. Halloween is a great excuse to create and wear a fabulous mask.

Although traditional masks are often made from wood, many other materials, including paper and card, papier mache, feathers, and leather, can also be used. They are often highly decorated and brilliantly colored. Even real teeth might be added, or maybe real horns from goats, deer, or cows.

Mask-making is something anyone can do. If you have grandchildren, they might like to try their hand at making masks. All you have to do is provide some materials and a little time. You might even decide to host a small party where wearing a mask is part of the fun, and there could be a competition for the most original mask on display.

SCRATCH ART

What is scratch art? You may know it as Art-foil, foil art, or even engraving art. And it is a little like engraving. Since you scratch off the black inky surface to reveal the color underneath, the results can be quite stunning.

Scratch art all started in England and France in the 19th century. Then, it was easy to reproduce as an alternative to metal wood or linoleum engraving, but now Mexico has developed a unique way of using it. The designs can be intricate, precise, and sometimes highly colored.

First, you scratch the top coat, usually black ink, but why not use different colors? The base may be white or multi-colored. Then, color can be painted on, and even that layer can be further scratched to make subtle changes to your pattern. Once complete, you will want to preserve your art by varnishing it, framing it, and hanging it.

Simple kits, for starters, are easy to find. When you get more skilled, you can paint in background colors, add glitter if you wish, and make unique pictures to adorn your walls.

TREE OF LIFE

The beautiful trees of life are pottery, artistic creations traditional to central Mexico. While pottery has been as long ago as 1800 BC, the tree of life has evolved over the centuries. The original clay figures were unpainted, but later color was added, and later still, the Christian religion influenced their design as a way to tell the stories of the bible. The Spanish priests destroyed images of the ancient gods, replacing them with Christian symbols.

The original Christian trees of life depicted the story of Adam and Eve and the Garden of Eden. Still, popular designs also included Noah, and the Ark. Modern trees of life can show many themes, including flowers, mermaids, the cosmos, Mexican dances, and animals.

A traditional Christian tree typically has an image of God at the top. Beneath him is the creation of the world in 7 days with the sun and moon, Adam and Eve, and the serpent. Finally, at the bottom, Adam is cast out of Eden.

The trees are made from clay and covered with small, brightly-colored, hand-painted images. The trees are usually between 26 and 60 cm tall, although there are some giant ones in public places. The clay is fired at low temperatures in gas ovens. A large one can take several years to complete, but the basic shape is somewhat like a candelabra, with arms to hold the tiny clay figures.

Every year there are competitions, including a 'Human Tree of Life.' In 2006, people from 63 ethnic groups dressed in native costumes and made a human pyramid. They had a message – peace in the world.

But how can you make this a hobby?

There are instructional videos on the internet for making them, but making the clay skeleton and figures in your kitchen would be hard. There are two alternatives:

You could buy one or collect a few and enjoy studying them. Read about them and decipher the stories behind them. Or you could make something similar from a card, paper, wire, glue, and paint. The old-fashioned pipe-cleaners make easy-to-make skeletons for small figurines. You could tell your own story and create your own Tree of Life, perhaps telling your own life story.

SUMMARY

As you can see, a great variety of hobbies are undertaken enthusiastically by the Mexican people. But color, brightness, and movement can be seen in all of them. The Jarabe dance tells a story. The masks illustrate stories, and the worry dolls create an excellent listening ear. So let your imagination go wild with the yarn or scratch art, and put everything together with a tree of life.

Jarabe Tapatio Dance
Yarn Art
Worry dolls
Masks
Scratch Art
Tree of life

PHILIPPINES

Why is the Philippines spelled with "ph," yet the people know themselves as Filipinos?

The name is derived from King Phillip the second of Spain, who reigned in the 16th Century. Spain was a seafaring nation whose sailors explored this area and instituted the Roman Catholic religion, which remains predominant today.

The Philippines consists of 7,641 islands. Over 5,000 islands still have no names on international maps, yet the Philippines make up the biggest archipelago in the world.

Filipinos know how to live a good life with family and friends, and music and singing are important elements of their way of life. The internet, skillfully used, plays a huge part as well. Many of their pastimes are social, from games such as basketball to wandering about the shopping malls.

So let us look more at some of the hobbies Filipinos enjoy.

KARAOKE

Singing is a national pastime; everyone loves to sing, whether they can or not!

Every opportunity to sing is enthusiastically taken. House parties, visitors to the home, and celebrations of all kinds are an excuse to sing; no reason is needed to burst into song. Children are surrounded by the sound of singing as they grow up and carry on singing as adults.

Karaoke has become a part of everyday life. Most Filipinos have a karaoke machine or a 'magic sing' microphone. This device makes your television a karaoke machine, easy to bring out when visitors arrive or parties are being hosted.

Legend says that karaoke began in Kobe in Japan. A certain band failed to turn up, so the bar owner was inspired to invite customers to take their place on the stage instead. The first karaoke machine was invented in Kobe when an orchestra went on strike, so the management substituted a machine.

You can find karaoke arcades along the streets in the Philippines, and these are popular places to visit in the evenings for a good sing-along. And no one minds if you are out of tune, it's the enthusiasm that counts.

Karaoke is a social activity, and once tried, it is fun for adults and children, and you can buy magic-sing equipment on the internet very easily. So, why not have a go? Invite a few friends around and have a ball.

PICNICS IN THE PARK

Eating out is about bonding with family and friends, and Filipinos always eat out.

With their warm weather and scenic parks, picnics are a natural way to spend time. And in the Philippines, there is one great advantage common to many Asiatic countries; one can find ready-prepared food in street stalls. So, it is easy to buy the food and take it to the nearest park to eat it. Moreover, the bought food is often cheaper than do-it-yourself cooking, as well as convenient.

However, when you make a barbeque, everyone has their share of the preparation, and everyone must wait for the meal to be ready. Nevertheless, it's an excellent way for family bonding, and Filipinos make the most of it. Indeed, cooking for Filipinos is about spending time with your family and doing something enjoyable together. And who doesn't enjoy good food and the outdoors?

In the Philippines, there is a particular word for just strolling outdoors – Lamyerda. Maybe with friends, perhaps time out for yourself, or simply an excuse to sample the delicious local ice-cream sorbets.

Have you tried taking a barbeque to your local park with your friends or family? Setting it up and cooking your favorite barbeque food? Some parks do not allow this, but most places permit it as long as you clear up afterward. A barbeque is a pleasant way to meet up with people you may not know very well or with your closest friends and family.

MALLING

What is 'malling?'

Malling means hanging out in the shopping mall. Malling is a serious business in the Philippines. There are about 865 malls, and each acts as a 'mini-economy.' Some of these malls are gigantic.

The malls are air-conditioned, which makes a pleasant break from what might be a hot and humid day. Filipinos go to the malls to cool down and meet their friends who are also escaping the heat.

And there is plenty to interest you. Window shopping, checking out the latest fashions, buying presents, or even just a pleasant walk. And if you get a bit peckish, you can find stalls selling local dishes or restaurants to rest your aching feet. Be warned; if you visit the Philippines, you may need to buy an extra suitcase.

Some of the special Filipino items for sale or display include pearls, silk, and baskets. Bamboo articles are popular, and specialist Barako coffee beans are worth sampling.

Have you explored your local mall? Maybe you have to drive a little distance to find one? Have you chatted to any of the vendors and sampled their wares? Have you ever eaten at the mall or met friends for coffee or lunch? Or have you ever simply been there wandering about amidst the bustle without any clear aim in mind? If the weather is poor, malling is a great way to get exercise and stay dry.

BASKETBALL

Basketball – is the most popular sport in the Philippines.

Taught at school, played after school in the alleyways and street corners, and encouraged in the gyms, basketball is followed by almost everyone in the Philippines. Everyone knows the rules, and most Filipinos are avid followers of the sport. In fact, according to Nike, they sell more of their sportswear to the Philippines than anywhere else except the USA and China.

A sport requiring little equipment makes this game accessible to everyone, young and old, rich and poor. You can sit at home or join a group in a club or bar and watch it, or, if you are active, you can join a team and participate. Maybe you have family members who are on a team you can support?

So important is basketball to Filipinos that elections might be postponed if they clash with the National Basketball Association (NBA) Finals. And, of course, you can follow the game live on television. A fast-action, fun-filled sport, it's easy to get involved and cheer for your team.

You could get interested in watching basketball on television if there is no team playing near you.

SOCIAL MEDIA

The Philippines is known as the 'text capital of the world' because of the massive number of text messages sent.

The figures are staggering. Filipinos use social media more than any other people worldwide, and the average user spends 11 hours a day on the internet. That's 60% more than the global average. Filipinos spend over four hours a day using social media.

Friendships are essential to Filipinos, so it's no surprise that Facebook is the most popular medium, with 99% of adults having Facebook accounts. But for influencers, Instagram and YouTube lead the way, with Facebook and Twitter also popular. Filipinos know that the people you know are the most valuable tool for getting on in life.

The Filipino people are avid readers and write blogs and upload photos and videos. In fact, this is where people know how to get the most out of the media, to understand the enormous benefits and the ways it can enhance your life.

Do you understand computers and smartphones? Are you taking advantage of the many benefits available? And importantly, are you also protecting your online presence?

SUMMARY

Laughter and singing, socializing in person and over the internet, and family and friends make for an energetic yet balanced way of life. Karaoke is everywhere, and picnics and barbeques in the park are popular. Basketball and malling are two somewhat different ways to have fun, and social media is a way of life in the Philippines.

Karaoke
Picnics in the Park
Malling
Basketball
Social media

THE UNIVERSAL HOBBY

Our final hobby is a challenge!

It has been gratifying exploring various countries and plucking out activities older people do in their spare time.

Almost everywhere, people play football, watch television and read. Some countries have hobbies that are so unique to the country that they cannot be exported, such as cheetah walking and wadi trails.

Here is your challenge. Can you find more countries with unique hobbies that one could do or modify to enjoy at home? Of course, they must be suitable for older people, not too expensive and must not entail visiting that country.

There are about 195 countries worldwide, so there is plenty to choose from. If you are interested in populations, you can watch the changes as they happen at: https://www.worldometers.info/.

I hope you have enjoyed your journey through 21 countries and that you feel inspired to try out a new hobby or two.

FINAL THOUGHTS

This has been another whirlwind adventure around the globe; discovering, learning, and pondering new hobbies to try at home. Hobbies worldwide are varied and often show a fascinating insight into the history of that country and the people living there.

Even if you cannot replicate the exact hobby, hopefully, it has given you ideas for engaging activities and crafts to inspire your next project. While some of these hobbies might appear less unique, they may be a reminder of an activity you once loved that you could participate in again? So, how might you adjust or refresh this hobby to suit you at this present time?

For many, touring the world is not an option due to the high cost of travel, or maybe your mobility is not what it once was. On the other hand, for some, reading about all these far away places might have you planning your next trip. Either way, I hope that the pages of this book have energized you, even if in some small way.

As discussed in the last chapter, perhaps you are now curious to research more hobbies from around the world? With about 195 countries globally, there is still a lot of territory to cover.

With your new finds, feel free to write to me and let me know what you've discovered so I can consider that hobby in a future book. You may reach me at:

ravina@ravinachandra.com, and I look forward to hearing from you.

INDEX

Acrylic fluid mountain art, Chapter 12, Nepal
Amateur archeology, Chapter 18, Egypt
Ankle bone games, Chapter 4, Mongolia
Archery, Chapter 4, Mongolia

Backgammon, Chapter 6, Turkey
Basketball, Chapter 21, Philippines
Basket weaving, Chapter 7, Oman
Basketry, Chapter 19, Zimbabwe
Beadwork, Chapter 19, Zimbabwe
Book-binding, *see Coptic book-binding*
Build your own yurt, Chapter 4, Mongolia
Burns night, Chapter 8, Scotland

Cake decorating, *see Samoan cake decorating*
Cats and Turks, Chapter 6, Turkey
Chilean music, Chapter 9, Chile
Chilean ice cream (and other desserts), Chapter 9, Chile
Christmas markets, Chapter 10, Croatia
Clog carving, Chapter 17, Liechtenstein
Coffee culture in Sweden, Chapter 2, Sweden
Coffee and tea Turkish style, Chapter 6, Turkey
Comedy, *see Irish comedy*
Composing, *see Poetry composing*
Coptic book-binding, Chapter 18, Egypt
Create your own designs and mood boards, *see Design and mood board creation*

Croatian palačinke crepes, Chapter 10, Croatia
Crocheting, Chapter 15, South Africa
Cross-country skiing, Chapter 14, Estonia
Crossword creation, Chapter 15, South Africa
Curry making, see Indian curry making

Dembee, Chapter 4, Mongolia
Design and mood board creation, Chapter 1, India
Döstädning, Chapter 2, Sweden
Duck herding, Chapter 3, Ireland

Felting, Chapter 12, Nepal
Fencing, Chapter 5, South Korea
Fermented shark, Chapter 11, Iceland
Fine mats, *see 'Ie toga*
Flags and their stories, Chapter 9, Chile
Fluid art, *see Acrylic fluid mountain art*
Folk music, Chapter 5, South Korea
Foreign language learning, Chapter 5, South Korea

Genealogy, Chapter 11, Iceland
Golf, Chapter 13, Jamaica
Gurning, Chapter 8, Scotland

Halawet Ahmad dessert making, Chapter 7, Oman
Highland fling, Chapter 8, Scotland
Hiking, Chapter 5, South Korea
Hobby, Chapter 8, Scotland
Hobby hunting, Chapter 22, Universal
Home beer brewing, Chapter 8, Scotland
Horses, *see Tiny horses*
Hieroglyphics, Chapter 18, Egypt

Hunting UFOs, *see UFO hunting*

'Ie toga (Fine mats), Chapter 16, Samoa
Indian curry making, Chapter 1, India
Internet, Chapter 14, Estonia
Irish comedy, Chapter 3, Ireland
Irish fairies and leprechauns, Chapter 3, Ireland

Jarabe Tapatio dance, Chapter 20, Mexico
Jerk sauce and ackee & saltfish, Chapter 13, Jamaica
Jukskei, Chapter 15, South Africa

Karaoke, Chapter 21, Philippines
Kite flying, Chapter 1, India
Kilikiti (Samoan cricket), Chapter 16, Samoa
Knitting, *see Patterns in knitting*

Lagom, Chapter 2, Sweden
Language learning, *see Foreign language learning*
Leprechauns, *see Irish fairies and leprechauns*
Lördagsgodis, Chapter 2, Sweden

Macro photography, Chapter 17, Liechtenstein
Malling, Chapter 21, Philippines
Malva pudding, Chapter 15, South Africa
Mandala drawing, Chapter 1, India
Markets, *see Souk market exploration*
Masks, *see Mexican masks*
Mbira instrumental music, Chapter 19, Zimbabwe
Medieval towns, Chapter 14, Estonia
Mexican masks, Chapter 20, Mexico
Mexican yarn art, Chapter 20, Mexico

Mood boards, *see Design and mood board creation*
Muboora une dovi traditional dish, Chapter 19, Zimbabwe
Museum visits, Chapter 14, Estonia

Okey, *see Rummikub or okey*
Olive oil soap making, Chapter 6, Turkey
Online courses, Chapter 15, South Africa

Papyrus papermaking, Chapter 18, Egypt
Patterns in knitting, Chapter 11, Iceland
Photography, Chapter 10, Croatia
Picnics Nepal style, Chapter 12, Nepal
Picnics in the park, Chapter 21, Philippines
Pirates and their history, Chapter 13, Jamaica
Poetry composing, Chapter 9, Chile
Puppetry, Chapter 10, Croatia

Reggae, Chapter 13, Jamaica
Ribel, Chapter 17, Liechtenstein
Rummikub or okey, Chapter 6, Turkey

Samoan cake decorating, Chapter 16, Samoa
Samoan cricket, *see Kilikiti*
Samoan umu cooking, Chapter 15, Samoa
Sauces in Iceland, Chapter 11, Iceland
Sauna, *see Swedish sauna*
Scratch art, Chapter 20, Mexico
Senet, Chapter 18, Egypt
Shark, *see Fermented shark*
Shona sculptures, Chapter 19, Zimbabwe
Silversmithing, Chapter 7, Oman
Singing, Chapter 14, Estonia

Singing bowls, Chapter 12, Nepal
Soap making, *see Olive oil soap making*
Social media, Chapter 21, Philippines
Soda bread baking, Chapter 3, Ireland
Souk market exploration, Chapter 7, Oman
Stamp collecting, Chapter 17, Liechtenstein
Swedish sauna, Chapter 2, Sweden
Swimming, *see Water polo or swimming*

The Highland fling, *see Highland fling*
The Hobby, *see Hobby*
The Internet, *see Internet*
Tiny horses, Chapter 11, Iceland
Tea and coffee Turkish style, Chapter 6, Turkey
Tree of life, Chapter 20, Mexico

UFO hunting, Chapter 9, Chile
Umu cooking, *see Samoan umu cooking*

Wadi fun, Chapter 7, Oman
Watercolor painting, Chapter 3, Ireland
Water polo or swimming, Chapter 10, Croatia
Wire puzzles games, Chapter 4, Mongolia
Worry dolls, Chapter 20, Mexico

Yarn art, *see Mexican yarn art*
Yurt, *see Build your own yurt*

IMAGE CREDITS

Chile
UFO over Trees by ursatii from Getty Images, under the Canva Pro Content License.

Croatia
Christmas Markets by clubfoto from Getty Images Signature, under the Canva Pro Content License.

Egypt
Ancient Egyptian Hieroglyphics by wwing from Getty Images Signature, under the Canva Pro Content License.
Papyrus Artisan at work by siculodoc from Getty Images, under the Canva Pro Content License.

Estonia
Tallinn by RudyBalasko from Getty Images, under the Canva Pro Content License.

Iceland
Icelandic Horses by stannic from Getty Images, under the Canva Pro Content License.

India

Herbs and spices by Studio Doros from Getty Images, under the Canva Pro Content License.

Ireland (Éire)
Belgium Tervuren Herding Ducks by MereW322 Getty Images, under the Canva Pro Content License.

Jamaica
Spicy Grilled Jerk Chicken on a plate by from_my_point_of_view from Getty Images, under the Canva Pro Content License.

Liechtenstein
Stamp Collection by Blade_kostas from Getty Images Signature, under the Canva Pro Content License.

Mexico
Worry Dolls by elanneivy from Getty Images Pro, under the Canva Pro Content License.
Traditional Handmade Mayan, Mexican Mask by Maciejen Grabowicz from Getty Images, under the Canva Pro Content License.

Mongolia
Yurt in Mongolia by pascalou95 from Getty Images, under the Canva Pro Content License.

Nepal
Felt Flowers by agalma from Getty Images, under the Canva Pro Content License.

Oman
Spice Souk by cengizkarbakus from Getty Images, under the Canva Pro Content License.

Philippines
Smiling Sporty Filipina Female Basketball Player with Basketball by dtiberio from Getty Images, under the Canva Pro Content License.

Samoa
Wedding Cake Decoration by W Jayasinghe from Getty Images, under the Canva Pro Content License.

Scotland
Traditional Scottish Highland Dancing by Lucassek from Getty Images, under the Canva Pro Content License.

South Africa
Malva Pudding and custard by CarlaMc from Getty Images Signature, under the Canva Pro Content License.

South Korea
Sunrise at Jeju Do Seongsan Ilchulbong, Jeju Island by Noppasim Wongchum from Getty Images, under the Canva Pro Content License.

Sweden
Untitled by StockSnap from Pixabay, under the Canva Pro Content License.

Turkey
Stray cats in Turkey city by ValeriMak from Getty Images, under the Canva Pro Content License.

Zimbabwe
African men designing and producing beadwork by THEGIFT777 from Getty Images Signature, under the Canva Pro Content License.

PSSSST, DON'T FORGET YOUR FREE GIFT!

In **'4 Simple Steps to Create Your Perfect Morning Routine,'** you will discover:

- What a **morning routine** is and why it is essential you have one
- Why having a morning routine will bring you **more focus, productivity, and purpose to your life**
- The secret of creating a morning routine using these **four components** that will **align with your core values**
- How a morning routine can elevate your life so that you may live **vibrantly**, whether you are seeking a companion, exploring new interests, or improving your health

Go to www.ravinachandra.com/books to get it NOW

FROM THE AUTHOR

Thank you so much for reading *101 Ways to Enjoy Retirement* and *101 More Ways to Enjoy Retirement*. Please don't forget to write a brief review wherever you purchased this book. I am grateful for all feedback and your review will help other readers decide whether to read this book too. Follow this link to leave a review:

Interested in staying in touch to hear about any of my future books or projects? Would you like the opportunity to work with me directly in a personalized 90-day coaching program?

Contact me at ravina@ravinachandra.com

or visit www.ravinachandra.com

www.ingramcontent.com/pod-product-compliance
Lightning Source LLC
Chambersburg PA
CBHW031054080526
44587CB00011B/674